HUDDLED MASSES, MUDDLED LAWS

HUDDLED MASSES, MUDDLED LAWS

Why Contemporary Immigration Policy Fails to Reflect Public Opinion

Kenneth K. Lee

Westport, Connecticut
London

Library of Congress Cataloging-in-Publication Data

Lee, Kenneth K.
    Huddled masses, muddled laws : why contemporary immigration policy
fails to reflect public opinion / Kenneth K. Lee.
      p. cm.
    Includes bibliographical references and index.
    ISBN 0-275-96272-5 (alk. paper)
    1. United States—Emigration and immigration—Government policy.
2. United States—Emigration and immigration—Public opinion.
3. Immigrants—United States—Public opinion. 4. Public opinion—
United States. I. Title.
JV6483.L43 1998
325.73—dc21   98-11126

British Library Cataloguing in Publication Data is available.

Library of Congress Catalog Card Number: 98-11126
ISBN: 0-275-96272-5

First published in 1998

Praeger Publishers, 88 Post Road West, Westport, CT 06881
An imprint of Greenwood Publishing Group, Inc.

Printed in the United States of America

The paper used in this book complies with the
Permanent Paper Standard issued by the National
Information Standards Organization (Z39.48–1984).

10 9 8 7 6 5 4 3 2 1

To my mother and father
for all their sacrifices

Contents

Figures and Tables

FIGURES

TABLES

Preface

Immigration is a very "hot" political topic. In the past several years, both proimmigration and restrictionist writers have authored numerous books, many of which were best-sellers. Political journals have also devoted extensive attention to immigration as well. And this topic will likely remain a contentious issue as long as high levels of immigration continue. This brief book, however, is not intended as a polemic. It does not make any normative judgments about our immigration policy. This does not mean that I am agnostic on the subject. As an immigrant myself, I have my own personal opinions on immigration, but I have scrupulously avoided taking sides in this heated debate. Rather, this book objectively analyzes why our immigration policy fails to reflect the public opinion. Until the mid-1960s, public policy had almost always followed public opinion on the issue of immigration. Then public opinion became seemingly irrelevant. It is a perplexing question that very few people have asked or attempted to answer. The following pages will try to answer this policy conundrum.

This book could not have been possible without the patient help of dozens of people who agreed to be interviewed. They provided valuable insight on coalition-building tactics and other political strategies employed in the passage of the 1990 and 1996 immigration bills. Among the more helpful were former Senator Alan Simpson of Wyoming, Congressman Lamar Smith of Texas, Chamber of Commerce lobbyist

Peter Eide, Organization of Chinese Americans director Daphne Kwok, and FAIR Director of Research Skip Garling. Lobbyist Rick Swartz deserves a special thanks for all his help: not only did he talk to me on several occasions, but he also provided me with his strategy memos and personal correspondence from the 1990 and 1996 immigration policy battles.

Karl Zinsmeister, the editor of the *American Enterprise* magazine, receives my thanks for piquing my interest in immigration policy and trusting me so many times. Peter Collier also deserves my gratitude for taking a chance on me. I would also like to thank all of my professors and teachers at Cornell University and Harvard Law School. Jeremy Rabkin has been and continues to serve as an intellectual mentor-of-sorts for me. On a more personal note, Peter Hoegel, Zak Lafitte, and Richard Tung deserve my thanks for their continued friendship. Also, my family has always been there for me. In particular, my heartfelt gratitude goes to my parents for all their sacrifices.

Chapter 1

Introduction: The Immigration Puzzle

In July of 1989, the Commissioner's Task Force on Minorities presented to the New York Board of Regents a scathing study that excoriated the city's public school curriculum as culturally biased against nonwhite students. A major impetus for the creation of this task force had come from the rapidly changing ethnic stock of the city's schoolchildren: the large influx in recent decades of nonwhite students—most of whom immigrated from the Third World—raised questions about the inclusiveness of the schools' textbooks. The report, titled *A Curriculum of Inclusion: Report of the Commissioner's Task Force on Minorities: Equity and Excellence*, brashly declared that, "African-Americans, Asian Americans, Puerto-Ricans/Latinos and Native Americans have all been the victims of an intellectual and educational oppression that has characterized the culture and institutions of the United States."[1]

The controversial study also claimed that a "systematic bias" toward European culture in the city's public schools had miseducated nonwhite students.[2] The jeremiad continued: "The curriculum in the education system reflects . . . deep-seated pathologies of racial hatred. . . . Because of the depth of the problem and the tenacity of its hold on the mind, only the most stringent measures can have significant impact."[3] Task force member Harry Hamilton explained the ultimate goal of the task force to the New York Board of Regents, the organization responsible for state education policy: "We're on the brink of something very important for New York and the nation. We have to change the entire framework in the way we look at ourselves as a nation. Instead of one group, European Americans, at the head of a long table, with other cultures present only as invited guests, we will have a round table with all cultures equal."[4]

The task force's report drew the ire of many political pundits and social critics, who saw it as evidence of multiculturalism run amok. California superintendent of public education Bill Honig, for example, blasted the report as "nothing but racism."[5] One of the more vehement critics was Lawrence Auster, a New York-based free-lance writer. In a partial response to the task force's study, Auster penned a pamphlet titled *The Path to National Suicide: An Essay on Immigration and Multiculturalism* in 1990. As suggested by the strident and ominous title, it vigorously inveighed against America's generous immigration law. "Our current policy of open and ever-widening immigration, in conjunction with the gathering forces of cultural radicalism, is leading our country into an unprecedented danger," he wrote. "We are thus imperiling not only our social cohesiveness but . . . the very basis of our national existence."[6] He argued that mass immigration was balkanizing America. The divisive debates over multiculturalism and bilingualism were the bitter fruits that America's immigration policy had sown. Indeed, according to Auster, New York City's controversial curriculum was a prime example of how immigration was unraveling the cultural fabric of America. Auster worried that the "browning" of America— caused primarily by high levels of immigration from the Third World— coupled with race-specific policies, would undermine the traditional Western basis of American society.

At the time of its publication, Auster's thin tome was largely unnoticed, partly because it was distributed by the American Immigration Control Foundation, a fringe anti-immigration group.[7] Since its publication in 1990, Auster's polemic has gone on to become a cult classic among restrictionists. Peter Brimelow, a senior editor at *Forbes* and one of the most outspoken critics of the current immigration policy, has compared Auster's pamphlet to Tom Paine's *Common Sense*.[8] Brimelow shared Auster's fear of cultural disintegration, and he wrote a widely noted front-cover article for the *National Review* in 1992.[9] Sometimes bordering on nativism but always engaging, Brimelow warned that whites would become a numerical minority within several decades if current demographic trends continued. Since the publication of

Brimelow's article, *National Review*, the pre-eminent journal of opinion among conservatives, has repeatedly published large pieces criticizing America's immigration policy.

At the same time that cultural conservatives like Auster and Brimelow were railing against mass immigration, many political liberals were expressing doubts as well. Richard Lamm, then the Democratic governor of Colorado, called for a dramatic reduction in legal immigration in his coauthored book, *The Immigration Time Bomb*.[10] Fearing that high levels of immigration depressed wages and displaced American workers, he sternly warned, "The United States cannot try to solve the world's unemployment problems by absorbing the world's unemployed."[11] And Lamm, though hardly a conservative, believed that the great expansion of the welfare state during the 1960s made it more likely that today's immigrants would be a burden on taxpayers. Among liberal politicians and policy wonks, this strain of anti-immigration thought is supported by the likes of Lamm, Representative Dick Gephardt and *The New Republic* senior editor John J. Judis.

Anti-immigration politicians and popular journals found much of their ammunition in academia. Many economists argued that the labor market could not sustain high levels of immigration. Among the more prominent critics was Vernon Briggs, a labor economist at Cornell University. He maintained that immigrants depressed wages and took jobs away from low-skilled workers, especially African-Americans. "Immigration supplies workers without regard to the macro human resource needs of the economy," he argued.[12]

Politicians and academics were not alone in their criticisms. Polls since 1965 consistently show that Americans share their reservations. Indeed, Americans have always felt some ambivalence toward immigration. The United States may be a nation of immigrants, but nativism is also very much a part of American history. From the colonial period until the end of the nineteenth century, America had virtually no substantive limits on immigration, and, in fact, it was actively encouraged. By the end of the nineteenth century, however, America slowly erected barriers, and immigration had come to a near halt by 1924. These limitations lasted until the booming economy and the racial liberalism of the 1960s led to the Immigration Act of 1965, which abolished the ethnocentric national origins quotas and instead established family-reunification as the main criterion for admission into America.

Soon after the passage of the Immigration Act of 1965, opposition to immigration spiked up. The act had the unintended consequence of increasing immigration dramatically. In the year before the passage of this seminal legislation, about 290,000 immigrants came to America. By the 1980s, the United States was allowing in nearly one million immigrants and refugees each year—the highest since the turn of the century (see fig. 1.1). And if illegal immigrants, whose actual numbers are nebulous, are counted into the figure, the United States is almost definitely accepting more immigrants than ever before in its history (although immigrants as a percentage of the general population was higher during the late nineteenth century).

The ethnic character of immigrants has also changed since 1965. In 1994, only 20% out of the 800,000 immigrants who entered the United States came from Europe.[13] In the decade prior to the enactment of the 1965 law, Europeans had represented a majority of the immigrants (see fig. 1.2). This massive increase in Third World immigration has raised doubts about the assimilability of these newcomers. These doubts are reflected in the polls. Since 1965, no more than 9% of the people polled want to increase the level of immigration, while since 1981, the majority of people want to reduce immigration levels.[14]

Yet, in recent decades, public policy has rarely reflected public opinion on the issue of immigration. At the same time that Professor Briggs and Lawrence Auster were warning about the dangers of the current levels of immigration, Congress was busily crafting the Immigration and Naturalization Act of 1990, the first major legal immigration legislation since 1965. The 1990 act actually *increased* the annual number of immigrants by nearly 40%. This congressional action was all the more surprising because a Roper poll—taken only four months before the passage of the Immigration and Naturalization Act of 1990—revealed that most people opposed increased immigration.

Why is there this disparity between public policy and public opinion? Why has the federal government ignored and even flouted the wishes of the people? What is the link between legal and illegal immigration policies? These are important questions because immigration intersects with the most contentious issues of our time, such as welfare, race, multiculturalism, bilingualism, unemployment and the plight of African Americans. Not surprisingly, immigration is becoming one of the most hotly debated issues of our time. Already, countless articles and books have debated the merits and demerits of immigration. And political journals have staked their positions. *National Review*, the flagship

Figure 1.1
Number of Immigrants Entering the U.S., 1820–1990 (by Decade)

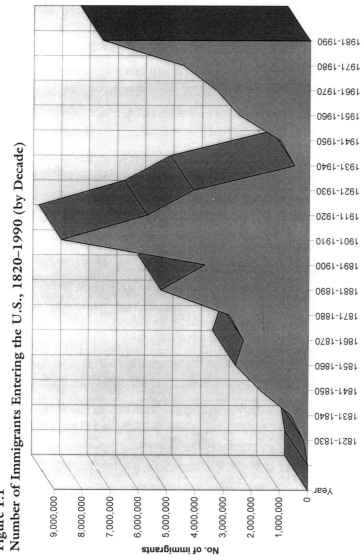
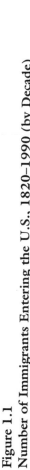

Source: Adapted from U.S. Immigration and Naturalization Service. *Statistical Yearbook of the Immigration and Naturalization Service, 1994.* (1996).

Figure 1.2
Immigrants Admitted by Geographic Region, 1955–1990

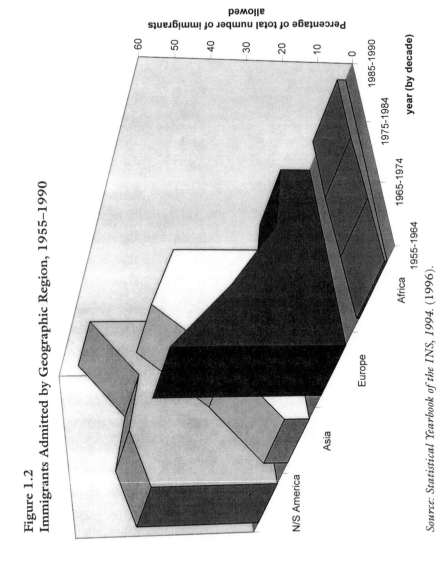

Source: Statistical Yearbook of the INS, 1994. (1996).

magazine of the Right, has crusaded for drastic reductions in immigration, while other journals, such as *Commentary* and *The New Republic*, have remained, on the whole, staunchly pro-immigration. Immigration is a hot issue among policymakers and politicians, too. Anti-immigration rhetoric has found a home among populist politicians like Pat Buchanan and Ross Perot. Buchanan garnered extensive media coverage during the 1996 primary season by peppering his speeches with pejorative references to illegal aliens named "José."[15]

Amid all this cacophonous debate, little attention has been paid to how immigration laws have been constructed since 1965. This brief book will try to fill in this gap by examining how post-1965 immigration laws have been created in light of the hostile public opinion. Note, however, that this is not a normative study on the impact of immigration. Before we debate whether we should increase, decrease, or maintain current levels of immigration, we should at least know how our laws have been created.

Some skeptical readers may point out that this divergence between public opinion and policy occurs in myriad issues—for example, on gun control. They argue that congressional representatives pay more attention to powerful interest groups than to inattentive constituents.[16] This observation is undoubtedly true to some extent; in a pluralist republic like ours, representatives do not follow every whim of a fickle electorate, especially on arcane issues that most voters have little knowledge about or that impose minimal costs on the electorate. Nevertheless, public policy usually does not diverge from public opinion for an extended period of time on an emotionally charged issue like immigration. Several studies have shown that public opinion does matter. Political scientists Benjamin I. Page and Robert Y. Shapiro examined several hundred public opinion polls from 1935 to 1979 and chose 357 salient issues that were mentioned repeatedly in surveys and showed changes in opinions.[17] They then examined policy changes for the two years before the poll was conducted and up to four years after the last survey on that question. After examining the data, Page and Shapiro concluded, "The finding of substantial congruence between opinion and policy (especially when changes are large and sustained, and issues are salient), together with the evidence that opinion tends to move before policy more than vice versa, indicates that opinion changes are important causes of policy change. When Americans' policy preferences shift, it is likely that congruent changes in policy will follow."[18] Contrary to complaints that our government does not follow the public's wishes, our elected representatives effectively reflect the views of the electorate on most issues—but not so for immigration.

In the past, public policy on immigration *did* follow public opinion. When the public expressed disapproval over immigration, the United States had no reservations about placing draconian restrictions. From 1921 to 1965, immigration was severely limited from most parts of the world. Ironically, the rationale for restricting immigration seems stronger today than in the past, if we consider the host of new complicating factors, such as the advent of the welfare state, the rise of identity-politics that stress the importance of racial separatism, and overpopulation.

This divergence between public opinion and policy is more perplexing if we consider that the American government today is arguably the most plebiscitary in our history. Many of the intermediary structures that have traditionally mediated the coarse views of the electorate have been gradually eliminated. Contrary to popular rhetoric, we live in a republic, not a democracy. The framers of the constitution feared that mass participation would lead to demagoguery and intemperate decisions. In a candid criticism of direct democracy, James Madison in *Federalist Paper* Number 49 warned that, "Frequent appeals would, in great measure, deprive the government of that veneration which time bestows on everything, and without which perhaps the wisest and freest governments would not possess the requisite stability."[19] The framers instead established a republic where representatives would "filter" the crude and simplistic opinions of the masses. For example, the president was to be elected by the electoral college, the senators by state legislatures. Many of these intermediate structures, however, have frayed since the founding of the country. The electoral college today is nothing more than an archaic, symbolic system; the Seventeenth Amendment allowed the direct election of senators; religious clauses in state governments were eradicated; and suffrage has been greatly expanded to include women, racial minorities, and even eighteen-year-olds.

Recent scholarship on congressional politics affirms the importance of public opinion. "Legislators adjust their behavior in office to avoid electoral problems, and they do this by paying careful attention to the known preferences of attentive publics and the potential preferences of inattentive citizens," writes political scientist R. Douglas Arnold.[20] He notes that representatives gauge the opinions of even inattentive citizens because they fear that political challengers or interest groups can publicize potentially unpopular votes. Consequently, congressional representatives have staff members who offer service to constituents and diligently keep track of their opinions on pending legislation. It does not take much imagination to recognize the potential political points that a congressional challenger can earn from exploiting raw anti-immigration sentiments.

In short, public opinion has a powerful effect on public policy. Returning to the example of gun control, the public wish finally came to fruition in 1993 with the passage of the Brady bill, despite opposition from possibly the most powerful interest group in America, the National Rifle Association.[21] The same does not apply for immigration. For nearly three decades, the Congress and the president—whether it be Ronald Reagan or Bill Clinton, the Gingrich-led Congress or a Democratic Congress—have not implemented any immigration restriction reform. In fact, when Congress finally acted in 1990, it surprisingly did the exact opposite of the public's wishes and increased legal immigration by nearly half.

Why has public policy failed to reflect public opinion on immigration in recent decades? Fortuitous historical changes have weakened the power of the restrictionist groups vis-à-vis the proimmigration forces. First, the civil rights zeitgeist exacted a powerful blow against nativist groups that had traditionally lobbied for restrictionism. It also empowered ethnic groups like the National Council on La Raza, which soon became major players in the Democratic Party. Secondly, the rise of conservative economics during the 1970s swayed many Republicans to support high levels of immigration as a way to keep America globally competitive. The power of ideas should not be underestimated. These two developments facilitated an unusual but powerful Left-Right coalition that defended high levels of immigration.

Yet even if a strong coalition of liberals and conservatives gets its way in Congress, proimmigration congressmen still have to face angry constituents when they go back home. Proimmigrationists have shrewdly shielded themselves from adverse public opinion in two ways. First, the surge in illegal immigration during the 1970s—which coincided with the increase in legal immigration—allowed legislators to divert the public's attention toward illegal immigrants, who do not have the same level of political clout as legal immigrants. By being tough on illegal immigration, proimmigration congressmen were able to insulate themselves from a potential public backlash. Second, proimmigration forces shrewdly reshaped the terms of the debate. Proimmigration groups were able to define immigration in terms of a valence issue like the "family." Restrictionist groups, not eager to argue against a sacro-sanct institution like the family, foundered in their attempts to curtail immigration.

This combination of a bipartisan coalition and Congress's shrewd diversionary tactics has prevented drastic reductions in legal immigration levels.

THEORIES AND IMMIGRATION POLICY

Since 1965, Congress has passed several key bills on immigration. This brief book will examine the three major pieces of legislation since 1965: the Immigration Reform and Control Act of 1986 (IRCA), the Immigration and Nationality Act of 1990 (INA), and the recently passed 1996 immigration bill (which was attached to a larger appropriations bill). The INA and the IRCA are the two most consequential and comprehensive immigration laws since 1965; the 1996 law is not as significant as the other two, but it is included because it is the only restrictionist bill to have received serious consideration in the past seven decades.

The IRCA (PL 99-603) was primarily an illegal immigration bill: It granted amnesty to several million illegal aliens who had been in the country since 1982; imposed sanctions on businesses that knowingly hired undocumented workers; and established temporary status visas for seasonal agricultural workers.[22] Although this book is mostly concerned with legal immigration, the IRCA nevertheless merits some attention. First, the original bills of the Immigration Reform and Control Act had placed a firmer cap on legal immigration, but that provision was expunged in the final version. Why and how this happened is noteworthy. Second, the dynamics between legal and illegal immigration will help explain the legal immigration policy puzzle.

The INA (PL 101-649) is the only full-fledged legal immigration law since 1965. The main provisions of the law included an increase in the national immigration level from about 500,000 to 675,000 people annually; a tripling in the number of business-related visas allotted on the basis of skills to 140,000; and the creation of a 55,000 visa "diversity" independent category for primarily Europeans whose numbers were adversely affected by the 1965 law.[23]

The 1996 immigration law, like the IRCA, concerns itself only with illegal immigration. It contained a smorgasbord of provisions to deter illegal immigration, ranging from increased border patrol to expedited deportation procedures.[24] Both the House and Senate versions originally had provisions to reduce legal immigration by a third, but these clauses were ultimately stripped, and the bill only focused on illegal immigration. How and why this occurred needs to be explained.

Scholarly works on the formation of recent immigration law are relatively sparse, but several theoretical models of public policy have been applied to elucidate the formulation of immigration policy. Though none is completely convincing, each adds some nuance to the bigger picture. What follows below is a short synopsis of three major theories of public policy. It is not intended as a complete or thorough analysis; rather, it is intended briefly to familiarize the reader with these theories to help explain our immigration policy conundrum.

Perhaps the most common and classic theory of policy-making is the pluralist theory. The pluralist view argues that policy is made by societal groups that compete and bargain with each other in pursuit of their own individual interests. This theory's antecedent lies in James Madison's famous *Federalist Paper* Number 10. While Madison saw factions as a necessary evil that was "adverse . . . to the permanent and aggregate interests of the community," modern pluralist theory often treats competition among interest groups as an inherent good.[25] Robert Dahl and David Truman are modern proponents of the pluralist theory.[26] The pluralist framework has several assumptions: (1) political problems involve primarily the allocation of goods; (2) the state acts as an "empty box" where interest groups compete; the state itself is not autonomous; (3) all groups have equal access to the political arena; (4) but some groups have more resources—in wealth, information, and the like—so they may have more influence in the policy-making process; and (5) individuals coalesce around common goals, and the policy outcome is the political equilibrium that results from the competition and bargaining among different groups.[27]

It should be noted that more subtle pluralist theories recognize the primacy of business groups in the political arena. As political scientist Charles Lindblom puts it, "Businessmen generally and corporate executives in particular take on a privileged role in government that is, it seems reasonable to say, unmatched by any leadership group other than government officials themselves."[28] In a market-based economy, the government must be solicitous to the needs of businesses because the general welfare of the country depends on their productivity. Wealth, however, is not the only criterion for influence. A group can

have other resources such as information, organization, and persua-
siveness that may significantly influence policy.[29] In this framework,
organized groups, not the undifferentiated public, are the primary
players. A pluralist interpretation of immigration policies would explain that our laws have been shaped by the competition, interaction,
and bargaining among interest groups. Thus, the inability to restrict
immigration is caused by the overwhelming strength of proimmigration groups vis-à-vis restrictionists.

Another prevalent model, the elite theory, repudiates the pluralist
notion of numerous groups competing and vying for political advantage. Instead, an elite group or class dominates the policy arena. Most
elite theories are rooted in neo-Marxism or class-analysis, and emphasize big business's hegemony: a coterie of advanced capitalists tailor
policies that are beneficial to this elite class, while the interests of the
working class are largely ignored. As social scientist C. Wright Mills
explains, "The power elite is composed of men whose positions enable
them to transcend the ordinary environments of ordinary men and
women; they are in positions to make decisions having major consequences."[30] Members of the elite usually posses wealth, but they share
other similarities, such as educational background and social charac-
teristics. A class-based elite theory would argue that capitalists have
erected generous immigration laws to provide cheap labor and depress
wages.

Like the pluralist theory, the elite model has subtle variations.
Instrumentalists see the state as a tool of the capital-holding classes,
while structuralists hold a less direct view, seeing the state as more
autonomous and arguing that the working class may occasionally "win"
to maintain the legitimacy of the system.[31] The difference between
pluralist and elite theories lies mostly in their emphasis. Elite theorists
believe in the primacy of capitalists, while pluralists argue that capitalists—while admittedly influential—do not have the dominance intimated by elite theorists, and that groups are better defined by their
behavior and self-definitions rather than by class position.[32]

Finally, there is the state-as-actor/realist approach, which emphasizes the autonomous feature of the state. The state is not a mere umpire
of different group interests, but rather an actor itself. Political scientist
Theda Skocpol explains, "States . . . may formulate and pursue goals
that are not simply reflective of the demands or interests of social
groups, classes or society."[33] This theory does not imply that interest
groups or class interests do not exist; rather, it argues that the state can

be an actor in the policy-making arena. Thus, the state-as-actor approach may posit that our immigration laws are based on foreign-policy considerations of the president. The validity of all three theories will be examined in subsequent chapters.

In addition to all these theories, one must also take into account the political and historical culture of the United States. America has a unique tradition of being a nation of immigrants. Even those who oppose increased immigration, at least, give lip service to the contributions that immigrants have made to America. This "immigration mystique" is especially prevalent among policymakers. Although America rarely accepted immigrants with open arms, this mystique has been ingrained into our political culture. In speech after speech on the floor of Congress, congressmen have paid homage to their immigrant ancestors. History and tradition play a substantial but relatively unappreciated role in immigration policy.

Interest groups also feel compelled to at least show some veneration for immigration: invited speakers at congressional hearings usually praise immigrants or stress that they are not in any way motivated by nativism. Thomas Donahue of the AFL-CIO prefaced his remarks by saying that he is in "no sense anti-immigration or anti-immigrant."[34] Or take Doris Meissner of the Carnegie Endowment for International Peace, who warned against increasing immigration, but still felt obliged to note that, "Historically, immigration has played a central role in the U.S. economy."[35]

In light of this immigration mystique, policymakers have instead directed most of their animus toward illegal immigrants, who do not enjoy the same historic mantle of veneration or strong interest group representation as legal immigrants. Yet this emphasis is not based purely on political expediency. Illegal immigration, by definition, is illegal and thus requires more immediate attention. And by fortuitous circumstance, illegal and legal immigration spiked up during the 1970s and 1980s, hampering legal immigration reform. Both the 1986 and 1996 laws started out with firmer caps on legal immigration, but ended up establishing stern provisions against illegal immigration instead. The 1986 law, in particular, is a great example of interest group politics: it expunged provisions limiting legal immigration and granted amnesty to millions of illegal immigrants who provide labor to agri-businesses (but Congress pledged to be harsh against a "phantom" enemy of illegal aliens who have not yet arrived in the United States). This linkage between illegal and legal immigration helps explain why public policy fails to reflect public opinion.

IMMIGRATION TODAY

How do immigrants come to the United States today? America's system of immigration law can be Byzantine and confusing to the uninformed observer. Congressmen and interest groups representatives will routinely bandy about esoteric terms like "fifth preference immigrants" and "pierceable caps." To understand fully what legislators are discussing and to comprehend the politics of immigration, it is important to know the basic structure of our current law. The reader can briefly thumb through this section's policy minutiae, but it is nevertheless important to know how an immigrant can come to the United States today.

The basic framework of our immigration policy was established by the 1965 Immigration Act, though the preference levels and quotas were adjusted by various subsequent legislation, most notably the 1990 act. The 1965 act created a seven-level preference system with 74% of the visas going toward family reunification, 20% for skills-based immigrants and 6% for refugees. It also established a worldwide cap of 290,000 annual immigrants and a 20,000 per-country limit, but immigration levels routinely exceeded the ceiling because "immediate relatives" (i.e., spouses, children, and parents of American citizens) are exempt from the cap. Thus, the total immigration level could and did exceed the "cap" of 290,000 (since 1965, an average of over 200,000 immigrants have entered annually under the immediate relatives category). Table 1.1 explains the different preference levels. The 1980 Refugee Act abolished the seventh preference level and gave the president more discretion over the number of refugees allowed in annually.

The 1990 Immigration Act altered the preference levels and remains as our current immigration policy. Overall, it set an annual permeable cap of 675,000 visas starting from fiscal year 1995. From 1992 to 1994, it set a level of 700,000 temporarily to ease backlogs. Within the 675,000 cap, the act allocated 480,000 visas for family-based purposes (71%), 140,000 for skills-based visas (21%), and 55,000 for independent "diversity" immigrants (8%) from primarily European countries adversely affected by the 1965 act. As dictated by the 1980 Refugee Act, refugees are exempt from the preference system.

Table 1.1
The Preference System as Established by the 1965 Act
(Was Effective until 1980)

Preference	Category	Number Allowed
First	Unmarried adult offspring of U.S. citizens	58,000 (20%)
Second	Spouses and unmarried offspring of permanent residents	58,000 (20%) [plus any not used in 1st preference]
Third	Professionals, scientists and artists of exceptional ability	29,000 (10%)
Fourth	Married offspring of U.S. citizens	29,000 (10%) [plus any not used in 1st/3rd preferences]
Fifth	Brothers and sisters of U.S. citizens	69,600 (24%) [plus any not used in first four preferences]
Sixth	Skilled and unskilled workers in areas with labor shortage	29,000 (10%)
Seventh	Refugees	17,400 (6%)
TOTAL	74% family-based, 20% skills-based, 6% refugees	290,000 (plus immediate relatives of U.S. citizens)

Source: Statistical Yearbook of the INS, 1994. (1996).

The apportionment of visas in the family-based category is complex and can be quite hairy. It set a pierceable cap of 480,000 for both family preference visas *and* the numerically exempt immediate relatives of U.S. citizens. Congress, however, feared that future increases in the numerically-exempt immediate relatives would take a larger portion of the 480,000 limit and eventually squeeze out the family preference visas. Thus, Congress set a minimum floor of 226,000 visas for family preference visas. So the 480,000 barrier can be "pierced" if there is an increase in the number of immediate relatives entering the United States. For example, if there were 300,000 immediate relatives in one year, the cap would be pierced to 526,000 to accommodate the minimum 226,000 visas for family preference visas. Table 1.2 details our current immigration policy.

The pierceable cap means that there really is no cap on legal immigration. Total annual immigration to the United States today

Table 1.2
Current Immigration Preference System as Set by the Immigration Act of 1990

Preference	Category	Number Allowed
FAMILY		*480,000*
First	Unmarried sons and daughters of U.S. citizens	23,400
Second	Spouses, children and unmarried offspring of permanent residents	114,200
Third	Married offspring of U.S. citizens	23,400
Fourth	Brothers and sisters of U.S. citizens (at least 21 years old)	65,000
	Immediate relatives of U.S. citizens	unlimited (but above 4 must be at least 226,000)
SKILLS-BASED		*140,000*
First	Priority workers	40,040
Second	Professionals w/ advanced degrees or exceptional ability	40,040
Third	Skilled workers, professionals, needed unskilled workers	40,040
Fourth	Special immigrants	9,940
Fifth	Investor visas	9,940
DIVERSITY		*55,000*
TOTAL	71% family-based, 21% skills, 8% diversity	**675,000** pierceable cap

Source: Statistical Yearbook of the INS, 1994. (1996).

routinely exceeds 675,000 because of the increase in the number of immediate relatives and refugees. In the 1990s, an average of 800,000 immigrants have entered the United States annually. This unabated stream of high levels of immigration has led to a strong public backlash against our current policy.

NOTES

1. Lawrence Auster, "The Regents' Round Table," *National Review*, 8 December 1989, p. 18.

2. "Understanding America's Diversity," *New York Times*, 16 February 1990, p. A34.

3. Auster, "Round Table," p. 19.

4. Ibid., p. 18.

5. Edward B. Fiske, "Lessons," *New York Times*, 7 February 1990, p. B5.

6. Lawrence Auster, *The Path to National Suicide: An Essay on Immigration and Multiculturalism* (Monterey, Va.: The American Immigration Control Foundation, 1990), p. 2.

7. The American Immigration Control Foundation is considered a pariah among the immigration circle. In 1990 the AICF circulated a poll that posed such tainted questions as, "Which of the problems associated with illegal aliens are the most personally disturbing to you? (check all that apply)." The choices were: "Taxpayer cost, Bilingual public education, Social Security fraud, Bring in diseases like AIDS, Drug trafficking and crime, Welfare fraud, loss of jobs for American citizens, other." AICF also received funds from the Pioneer Fund, a eugenics advocacy group. See Felix Perez, "Immigration poll is drawing fire as racist and inflammatory," *San Diego Union-Tribune*, March 25, 1990, p. C8.

8. Peter Brimelow, *Alien Nation: Common Sense about America's Immigration Disaster* (New York: Random House, 1995), p. 76.

9. Peter Brimelow, "Time to Rethink Immigration?" *National Review*, 22 June 1992, p. 30. The article is widely credited for pushing immigration onto the agenda of conservatives.

10. Richard D. Lamm and Gary Imhoff, *The Immigration Time Bomb* (New York: Truman Talley Books, 1985).

11. Ibid., p. 129.

12. Vernon M. Briggs, Jr., *Immigration Policy and the American Labor Force* (Baltimore: Johns Hopkins University Press, 1984), p. 45.

13. United States Immigration and Naturalization Service, *Statistical Yearbook of the Immigration and Naturalization Service, 1994* (Washington, D.C.: Government Printing Office, 1996), p. 21.

14. "Ambivalence toward Immigration," *American Enterprise*, March/April 1995, p. 105.

15. For example, see James Bennet, "Candidate's Speech is Called Code for Controversy," *New York Times*, 25 February 1996, sec. 1, p. 22.

16. For example, see Robert A. Bernstein, *Elections, Representation, and Congressional Voting Behavior: The Myth of Constituency Control* (Englewood Cliffs, N.J.: Prentice Hall, 1989).

17. Benjamin I. Page and Robert Y. Shapiro, "Effects of Public Opinion on Policy," *American Political Science Review* 22 (1983): 177.

18. Ibid., p. 177.

19. James Madison, Alexander Hamilton, and John Jay, *The Federalist Papers*, Clinton Rossiter, ed. (New York: Penguin, 1961), p. 314.

20. R. Douglas Arnold, "Can Citizens Control Their Representatives?" *Congress Reconsidered*, Lawrence C. Dodd and Bruce I. Oppenheimer, eds. (Washington, D.C.: Congressional Quarterly Press, 1993), p. 414. Also see R. Douglas Arnold, *The Logic of Congressional Action* (New Haven: Yale University Press, 1990).

21. Readers can probably think of other issues in which public opinion and policy diverge. The divergence, however, eventually closes for most prominent issues. In many race-based issues, such as affirmative action and school bussing, this divergence has persistently existed, but it can be explained by judicial action or executive fiat. Immigration levels, however, have almost never been adjudicated by courts; it is usually in the sole province of the democratic, political process. Finally, a divergence may exist if the issue is not salient or too arcane for people to understand or care about. For example, few people are knowledgeable enough about securities reform to have a definite opinion on it. Immigration—with its racial, cultural, and social welfare elements—is definitely not in this group.

22. *Congressional Quarterly Almanac 1986*, pp. 61–67.

23. *Congressional Quarterly Almanac 1990*, pp. 474–85.

24. Dan Carney, "As White House Calls Shots, Illegal Alien Bill Clears," *Congressional Quarterly Weekly Report*, 5 October 1996, p. 2864.

25. For the development of pluralist theory and how it has been transformed to view the competition among interest groups as intrinsically good, see Theodore J. Lowi, *The End of Liberalism: The Second Republic of the United States*, 2d ed. (New York: W. W. Norton & Company, 1979).

26. See Robert Dahl, *Who Governs?* (New Haven: Yale University Press, 1961), and David Truman, *The Governmental Process* (New York: Knopf, 1951).

27. Keith Fitzgerald, *The Face of the Nation: Immigration, the State, and the National Identity* (Stanford, Calif.: Stanford University Press, 1996), p. 37.

28. Charles Lindblom, *Politics and Markets: The World's Political-Economic Systems* (New York: Basic Books, 1977), p. 172.

29. Fitzgerald, p. 37.

30. C. Wright Mill, *The Power Elite* (New York: Oxford University Press, 1959), pp. 3–4.

31. Ibid., p. 43. For an instrumentalist view, see Ralph Miliband, *The State in Capitalist Society* (New York: Basic Books, 1969). For a structuralist thesis, see Erik Wright, *Class, Crisis, and the State* (London: New Left Books, 1978).

32. Fitzgerald, p. 47.

33. Theda Skocpol, *Bringing the State Back* (Cambridge: Cambridge University Press, 1985), p. 9.

34. U.S. Congress, House Subcommittee on Immigration, Refugees and International Law of the Committee on Judiciary, and Immigration Task Force of the Committee on Education and Labor, *Immigration Act of 1989 (Part I): Hearings*, 101st Congress, 1st Session, 1919, 423.

35. Ibid., p. 108.

Chapter 2

Public Opinion: What Americans Think about Immigration

In 1998 America will accept nearly one million immigrants, which is more than the immigrants to all other nations combined. Since 1607, when English immigrants first settled in Jamestown, Virginia, nearly 60 million people have come to America in search of political, religious and economic freedom.[1] The cliché that we are a nation of immigrants is indeed true, and most Americans do take pride in our country's unique history and role in the world. City districts like Little Italy and Little Saigon, booming with annual parades and bustling ethnic stores, are a testament to the country's immigrant heritage. But at the same time, Americans have usually opposed increased immigration. Native-born Americans have always feared that the newcomers will take their jobs away or lower wages and pose a fiscal burden on local governments. A nation that mythologizes Ellis Island and the Statue of Liberty ironically was once the home to the Know-Nothing Party and the National Origins Act. In short, Americans have historically felt ambivalent about immigration.

Although definitive public opinion polls date back only to the late 1950s, it is safe to say that anti-immigration attitudes hit their apogee during the 1920s and 1930s. Many factors were responsible for this restrictionist ethos. The abysmal economic condition of the 1930s and the isolation undercurrent factored heavily in the anti-immigration attitudes.[2] Also, nativism, shared by both the public and the elite policymakers, played a large role. Public policy reflected the public's restrictionist outlook as Congress passed the National Origins Act of 1924, which drastically limited immigration for the next four decades.

By the 1950s and 1960s, public attitude toward immigration had liberalized. Few Americans explicitly wanted to increase immigration, but opposition to it had abated markedly. A July-August 1965 Gallup poll revealed that only a third wanted to decrease immigration.[3] This change can be attributed to numerous factors, including a booming economy, the civil rights zeitgeist and foreign policy considerations in a Cold War era. Public policy reflected this change in public opinion with the passage of the liberalizing Immigration Act of 1965.

By the late 1970s, public opinion had shifted once again. A sluggish economy, unexpected mass immigration from the Third World, and the rise of the welfare state all helped push the public into the restrictionist camp. The desire to curtail immigration grew dramatically, from a third in the 1960s to up to two-thirds of those polled (see fig. 2.1). Virtually all the polls after 1980 show that at least a majority of the people support decreasing immigration. And some polls reveal that a large minority—about 20%—favor the extreme solution of a complete moratorium on immigration. Yet, for the first time in American history, public policy has not reflected this change in public opinion on immigration.

It should be noted that the public has almost never explicitly supported increasing immigration. The benefits of increased immigration are far too indirect and diluted over a large population for a substantial majority to want more immigrants to enter the country. Few people will actually contact their congressman to push for increased immigration. Rather, a better barometer for gauging the public opinion is the percentage of people who want to *decrease* immigration. When the social and fiscal costs of immigration enlarge (or seem to enlarge), the public will demand restrictions and start contacting their legislators. And as figure 2.1 shows, the percentage of people who want to restrict immigration has been steadily increasing since the passage of the 1965 Immigration Act.

RACE AND IMMIGRATION

A salient difference between the new restrictionist mentality and the previous waves is that opposition to immigration is less rooted in racial prejudice. A 1985 *Time* poll asked people if certain immigrant ethnic groups had created benefits or problems for the country (see fig. 2.2).

Figure 2.1
Public Opinion Polls on Immigration Levels, 1955–1994

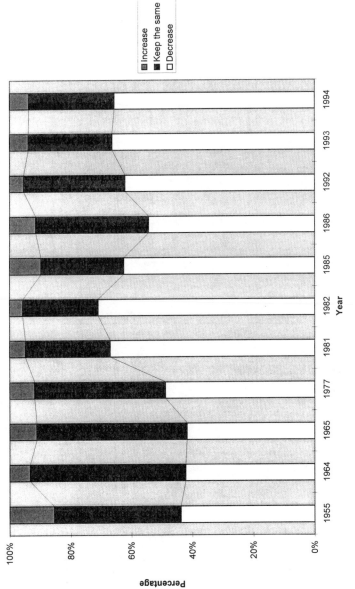

Source: Roper Center at University of Connecticut Public Opinion Online.

Figure 2.2
Have Immigrants Benefited the Country or Created Problems? (By Country of Origin)

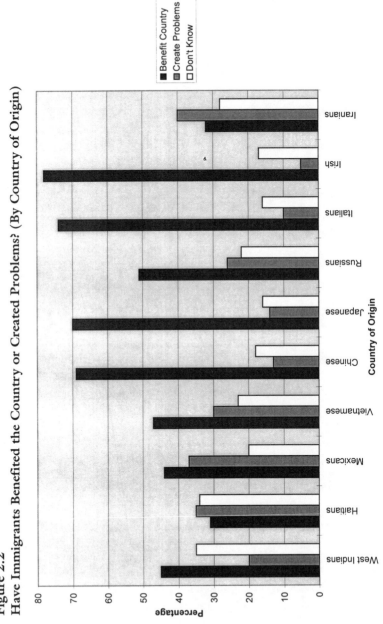

Source: Roper Center at University of Connecticut Public Opinion Online, *Time/Yankelovich Poll*, April 30, 1985.

Respondents were likely to see European immigrants in the most favorable light, but several nonwhite immigrants such as the Japanese and the Chinese had similarly high favorable ratings. The negative ratings for ethnic groups like the Mexicans may have less to do with race than with their lower socioeconomic status and, thus, their propensity to go on the public dole. And the high ratings for Europeans might be a feature of the predominantly European origin of the respondents. It would not be surprising if Irish Americans or Polish Americans held more favorable attitudes toward members of their own ethnic groups.

A 1984 poll conducted by Kane, Parsons and Associates also revealed similar results. The poll asked hypothetical situations using different ethnic groups, and most responses did not vary much by ethnicity.[4] For example, 82% thought that "a man from England who wants to come to the U.S. to be with his daughter who immigrated here ten years ago" should be admitted, while only 10% opposed it. The same question using instead a man from Taiwan revealed that 75% thought he should be admitted, while 16% did not. These poll numbers are salient for another reason. It shows how Americans, despite their restrictionist views, are supportive of immigration if it is framed in terms of family reunification because most Americans regard the family as paramount. As will be shown later, immigration supporters have effectively used this "soft spot" for the family to their advantage.

Some poll results seem to contradict this putative racial liberalism. One poll showed that 49% of the respondents thought that the United States was accepting "too many" immigrants from Asian countries, 31% for African countries, 53% for Latin America, and 26% for European nations.[5] Yet these results do not necessarily denote rank racial bias. Nearly 80% of today's immigrants come from Asia or Latin America, so it is not surprising if people believe that "too many" of them are accepted. It also may reflect the public's wariness over multicultural and bilingual public policies, which are legitimate concerns not necessarily coterminous with racism. Even liberal standard-bearers such as historian Arthur Schlesinger have voiced concern about muliticultural and bilingual policies, which have been implemented ostensibly for the benefit of Third World immigrants. Although people may favor immigrants from Europe, they nevertheless have racially liberal views in comparison to those held in earlier periods in history.

Views on immigration differ depending on which demographic group was polled (see table 2.1). Those who are black, less educated,

Table 2.1
Views on Immigration by Demographic Groups

In Favor of Halting Immigration	Percent
Education	
Grade School	81
High School	71
College	44
Race	
Black	79
White	64
Occupational categories	
Not labor force	74
Manual workers	73
Clerical and sales	68
Professional and business	48
Income level	
0-$5,000	78
5,000-9,999	78
10,000-14,999	72
15,000-19,999	59
20,000-24,999	60
25,000+	52

Source: Roper Center at University of Connecticut Public Opinion Online, Poll 1980.

work in blue-collar fields, or remain in the lower income bracket are more likely to favor halting immigration. These results are consonant with studies which show that "Formal education does not guarantee enlightenment, but it is a fundamental correlate of tolerance."[6] Self-interest also explains this correlation: the less well-off and the less educated are likelier to compete with immigrants for jobs, and thus will oppose immigration more vehemently. A corollary of this correlation is that congressional representatives—who are on the whole highly educated and had white-collar jobs before entering public office—are likelier to view immigration more favorably than their constituents do.

It is important to differentiate between public opinion on the level of immigration and on the character of immigrants. Although most Americans oppose high levels of immigration, they generally have favorable words for immigrants themselves. This is not as contradictory as it first may seem. It may be easier to hold harsher and more restrictionist views on an abstract notion like immigration level than toward specific people.[7] Two-thirds of Americans believe that immigrants "are productive citizens once they get their feet on the ground," and 58% believe that they are "basically good, honest people."[8] Furthermore, 74% believe immigrants do "menial work other people don't want to do" and a majority say they have made a "contribution to our country by enriching our culture." At the same time that Americans ascribe industriousness to immigrants, they also see them as a potential burden. The same poll showed that 61% thought immigrants "take jobs away from Americans," and 59% said they "end up on welfare." Those polled also saw other problems associated with immigration. Over half of the respondents, for example, said immigrants added to the crime problem. These widely diverging opinions show the ambivalence held by many Americans.

Though the public might be averse to current levels of immigration, its views are more sanguine from a historical perspective. Most Americans take pride in that we are a nation of immigrants. Most polls show that three-quarters of Americans say that we owe a great deal to immigrants, and 82% want a "national celebration" of immigrants.[9] And Americans love immigrant success stories: during the 1988 elections, three-quarters said they admired the not-so-popular Michael Dukakis for being the "first generation son of Greek immigrants who has worked hard to be a success."[10]

INTENSITY OF PUBLIC OPINION

How intense are these opinions? Most Americans believe that immigration is a very or fairly important issue, but it is not one of the top priorities, at least on a national level. A 1984 Gallup poll showed that 41% thought that immigration was a "very important" issue, while 31% believed it to be "fairly important."[11] A 1992 poll yielded similar results: 42% saw immigration as "very important," while another 44% said it was "moderately important."[12] To give some perspective on the intensity of opinion, immigration had roughly the same priority as the protection of the environment. The intensity of immigration views is relatively lower compared to issues considered to be "top priority." For example, public opinion on inflation in 1984 was one of the strongest, with 73% thinking it to be a "very important issue."[13] The issue of immigration, however, has gained increased saliency in the past few years. In 1992, 60% said they were "more concerned" about immigration than they were ten years ago.[14] The same poll showed that 72% thought that "sound leadership" on this issue was lacking, while only 13% thought there was "effective leadership."[15] And a 1994 poll said that 72% of the people believed that mass immigration constituted a "critical threat" to the "vital interest of the United States."[16] All these figures are from national polls; there are very few reliable regional poll data available. It is probably fair to assume that opposition to immigration is higher and more intense in states with a high foreign-born population because these states have to bear an unfair share of the costs of immigration (in terms of education, health care and social services provided) under our system of federalism.

What these poll results prove is that legislators, especially those from states with few immigrants, have some latitude in voting on immigration legislation because the public there does not see it as a top priority. However, they would find it politically dangerous to ignore the public's wishes once the issue goes on the national agenda. After all, it is difficult to imagine Congress gutting environmental regulations—which were considered to be of roughly the same priority as immigration—without facing serious political repercussions. When the Republican Congress tried to roll back environmental regulations in 1995, Democratic challengers effectively pounced on them. Furthermore, the fact that most people find "sound leadership" lacking means that legislators must heed the public even if the issue is relatively dormant, lest political challengers exploit it against them. Yet Congress has not heeded the public's wishes on immigration.

PUBLIC OPINION ON ILLEGAL IMMIGRATION

Most Americans erroneously think that illegal immigrants constitute the largest group of foreigners coming into the United States, although, in reality, three times as many legal immigrants enter the United States every year.[17] This ignorance on the part of the public allows proimmigration legislators to de-emphasize legal immigration reform and instead tackle illegal immigration as a way to cool the public's ardor. One can only guess how much more the opposition to legal immigration would increase if Americans knew the accurate numbers.

Public opinion has been consistently and adamantly opposed to illegal immigration since the 1970s. Illegal immigration increased dramatically during the 1970s, and the perception that it was a major problem was abetted by extensive media coverage of Cubans and Mexicans entering through Florida and California, respectively. Most Americans are opposed to illegal immigration on principle because it is, ipso facto, illegal. As a country that prides itself on the tradition of rule of law, we take umbrage at people who flagrantly violate our basic laws of national sovereignty. But the aversion to illegal immigration is rooted in more than just legal principle: most Americans also fear that illegal immigrants—more so than legal immigrants—will take away jobs and become a public burden. A *Los Angeles Times* poll showed that 62% thought that illegal aliens are a burden on the United States, while only 18% thought that they were beneficial.[18] For legal immigrants, the public is usually split fifty-fifty on these types of questions. Unlike legal immigrants, illegal aliens are seen in a negative light on both abstract *and* individual levels.

Opposition to illegal immigration has increased over the years. A Roper poll conducted in 1978 revealed that illegal immigration was considered the third largest cause (out of thirteen choices) of unemployment in America.[19] This impression is probably not based on reality: according to one poll, only 6% said that they had to compete with an undocumented worker for a job, and out of that subgroup, only 29% said they lost it to an illegal alien.[20] But what often counts in public policy is not reality, but perception.

The public's opinion on illegal immigration is relatively intense. In 1980, a whopping 91% thought that the United States should make an "all out effort" to stem the tide of illegal immigration.[21] And polls from 1981 to 1996 show that over half the American population see illegal immigration as a major problem (see fig. 2.3). In 1993, 85% thought that illegal immigration would become a "more serious problem" in the future.[22] And when asked what issues will be the most important to them in the 1994 elections, 20% answered illegal immigration (the top answers were crime at 33% and welfare reform at 28%).[23] Surprisingly, nearly half said that illegal immigration is one of the main reasons why they are "dissatisfied with the way things are going in this country."[24] These results are astonishing considering that these are national polls; opposition to illegal immigration is undoubtedly much higher in states like California, Florida, and Texas. Congressional representatives should feel this heat from their constituents: 84% of those polled said they wanted their representative to take a "leading national role" in finding ways to stop illegal immigration, and 65% were willing to spend more federal tax money to tighten the borders.[25]

Figure 2.3
Is Illegal Immigration a Major Problem/Very Important Issue?

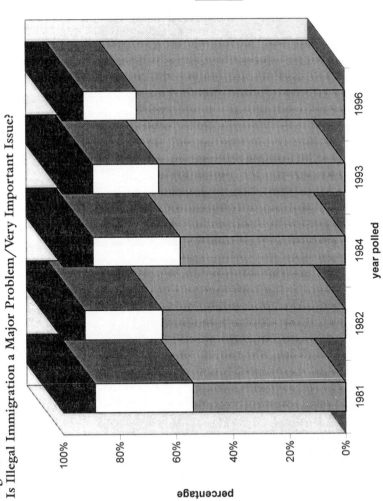

Source: Roper Center at University of Connecticut Public Opinion Online.

CONCLUSIONS

Since the passage of the Immigration Act of 1965, opposition to high levels of immigration has increased dramatically. What is most surprising is how the country has consistently wanted to decrease immigration since the 1960s. Today, nearly two-thirds of the people desire reductions in immigration. Yet today's opposition to immigrants is different from that of previous eras. Today, race no longer stands out as the main reason fueling the restrictionist movement: Americans have become more racially tolerant.

Notwithstanding the opposition to immigration, Americans have a soft spot in their hearts for families. When posed with a question about reuniting families, most Americans are willing to grant visas to reunite family members. As will be explained later, proimmigrationists have effectively used this generous attitude toward families to their advantage by centering the immigration debate around families, not numbers.

Any misgivings about legal immigration, however, are dwarfed by the universal opposition to illegal immigration. Most Americans incorrectly believe that illegal immigrants are the main source of foreigners into the United States and have little compassion for them. They view illegal immigrants, on both personal and abstract levels, with scorn, and the intensity of this opposition is very high.

NOTES

1. Rita J. Simon and Susan H. Alexander, *The Ambivalent Welcome: Print Media, Public Opinion and Immigration* (New York: Praeger, 1993), p. 3.

2. Edwin Harwood, "American Public Opinion and U.S. Immigration Policy," *Annals of the American Academy of Political and Social Sciences* 487 (1986): 203.

3. Ibid., pp. 202–203.

4. Roper Center at University of Connecticut Public Opinion Online, *Kane, Parsons and Associates*, Feb 2, 1984.

5. Roper Center at University of Connecticut Public Opinion Online, *Gallup/Newsweek*, May 9, 1984.

6. Harry Holloway and John George, *Public Opinion: Coalitions, Elites and Masses*, 2d ed. (New York: St. Martin's Press, 1986), p. 196.

7. Harwood, "American Public Opinion," p. 210.

8. Roper Center at University of Connecticut Public Opinion Online, *Roper/US News & World Report/CNN*, June 11, 1986.

9. Roper Center at University of Connecticut Public Opinion Online, *Time/Yankelovich, Skelly and White*, April 30, 1985.

10. Roper Center at University of Connecticut Public Opinion Online, *Harris Poll*, August 19, 1988.

11. Roper Center at University of Connecticut Public Opinion Online, *Gallup/Newsweek*, June 1, 1984.

12. Roper Center at University of Connecticut Public Opinion Online, *Roper/American Attitudes on Immigration*, March 27, 1992.

13. Harwood, "American Public Opinion," p. 208.

14. Roper Center at University of Connecticut Public Opinion Online, *Roper/American Attitudes on Immigration*, March 27, 1992.

15. Roper Center at University of Connecticut Public Opinion Online, *Roper/American Attitudes on Immigration*, March 27, 1992.

16. Roper Center at University of Connecticut Public Opinion Online, *Gallup/The Chicago Council on Foreign Relations*, October 7, 1994.

17. Roper Center at University of Connecticut Public Opinion Online, *Kane, Parsons and Associates/Public Attitudes toward Refugees and Immigrants*, February 2, 1984.

18. Roper Center at University of Connecticut Public Opinion Online, *Los Angeles Times Poll*, March 15, 1981.

19. Roper Center at University of Connecticut Public Opinion Online, *Roper Organization*, June 16, 1978.

20. Roper Center at University of Connecticut Public Opinion Online, *Los Angeles Times Poll*, March 15, 1981.

21. Roper Center at University of Connecticut Public Opinion Online, *Roper Organization*, June 5, 1980.

22. Roper Center at University of Connecticut Public Opinion Online, *Princeton Survey Research Associates/Newsweek*, July 29, 1993.

23. Roper Center at University of Connecticut Public Opinion Online, *NBC News/Wall Street Journal*, October 14, 1994.

24. Roper Center at University of Connecticut Public Opinion Online, *Princeton Survey Research Associates/Newsweek*, August 23, 1994.

25. Roper Center at University of Connecticut Public Opinion Online, *Roper/American Attitudes on Immigration*, March 27, 1992, and *Time/CNN/Yankelovich Partners, Inc.*, September 8, 1993.

Chapter 3

A History of Ambivalence

"Bosom of the America is open to receive not only the opulent and respectable stranger, but the oppressed and persecuted of all nations and religions, whom we shall welcome to a participation of all our rights and privileges," averred George Washington in 1783.[1] Nearly two hundred years later, another president—this time, Ronald Reagan—similarly intoned: "Can we doubt that only a divine Providence placed this land—this island of freedom here as a refuge for all those people in the world who yearn to be free?"[2] This idea of America as a nation of immigrants and a sanctuary for the oppressed has been echoed to the point that it has become a cliché. But for the most part, this cliché is accurate. No other country in the history of the world has attracted as many people from different parts of the world in such a short span of time. Indeed, America is one of history's few examples of a successful multiracial melting pot. From the first British colonists in the seventeenth century to today's immigrants from Latin America and Asia, people seeking economic and political freedom have sought out America.

Yet, contrary to popular folklore, immigrants have rarely been accepted with open arms. Although Americans proudly celebrate their immigrant heritage, they have also been historically ambivalent about immigration. Ironically, a country that mythologizes the Statue of Liberty was also once the home to the Know-Nothing Party and the

National Origins Acts. Table 3.1 details the varied history of American immigration policy. Some of the opposition to immigration was rooted in naked nativism and regnant racism; some of it based on legitimate fears of economic and cultural dislocation. Intermittently throughout America's history, restrictionists have succeeded in limiting immigration. American immigration policy can be categorized roughly into four periods: (1) the Open-Door Era (1700s–1880), when we had virtually unregulated immigration; (2) the Door-Ajar Era (1880–1920), when the U.S. established some limits; (3) the Restrictionist Era (1921–1964), when the U.S. enacted ethnically based national origins quotas and drastically reduced the flow of foreigners; and (4) the Dutch-Door Era (1965–present), when the family-reunification system opened the gates again.[3]

Interestingly, many of the arguments adduced by both restrictionists and immigrationists have not changed much since the colonial days. Scholars, politicians, and the general public all debated the economic impact of immigrants: Do they take away jobs from native-born Americans? Do they end up on the public dole? The political and cultural effect of immigration was discussed as well: Can immigrants assimilate into the American culture? What impact will they have on our political institutions? When the nation periodically asked itself these questions, the restrictionists often seemingly offered the better answers, and anti-immigration policies were consequently enacted. The country began to erect barriers against immigration in the late nineteenth century, and immigration came to a near halt by the 1920s when xenophobia and paranoia reached their apogee. This xenophobia was not always exclusively held by the Northern and Western Europeans. When the first large wave of immigrants from Southern and Eastern Europe came at the end of the nineteenth century, it was primarily Americans of Western and Northern Europe heritage who feared the infusion of Catholics and called for limits on immigration. Yet many black Americans, such as Booker T. Washington, also wanted restrictions because they saw the newcomers as added competition for jobs. Washington implored white Americans to hire blacks over recent European immigrants. Then, when Asians and Latinos started coming to America in the 1960s, it was often the Southern and Eastern European ethnics who strenuously opposed immigration and wanted to maintain racially biased immigration laws in our books. And, ironically, public opinion polls today reveal that many Asian Americans and Latinos want to close the borders now that they have made it to the

Table 3.1
Notable Immigration Policy Developments (1876–1996)

1876	In *Henderson v. Mayor of New York*, a federal court forbids states from regulating immigration.
1819	For the first time, the U.S. Government counts the number of immigrants.
1875	The federal government prohibits prostitutes and convicts from entering the U.S.
1882	Congress enacts the Immigration Act of 1882, excluding an assortment of undesirables: lunatics, idiots, people likely to become "public charges." The government also places a head tax on immigrants and prohibits Chinese immigration.
1885	Congress prevents contract laborers from immigrating.
1891	Ellis Island opens as an immigrant processing center.
1903	Polygamists and political radicals are added to the list of undesirables.
1907	Japan agrees to limit its number of immigrants to the U.S. in the Gentlemen's Agreement. Congress establishes the Dillingham Commission to study immigration.
1917	Overriding President Wilson's veto, Congress requires a literacy test. It also virtually bans all immigration from Asia.
1921	The Immigration Act of 1921 limits the number of immigrants from each country to three percent of that nationality's population in the U.S. in the 1910 census. European immigration is capped at about 350,000.
1924	The National Origins Quota system is solidified permanently: annual quotas is set according to the 1890 census. Non-Western Hemisphere country is limited to 150,00 each year.
1942	Bowing to pressure from growers during the labor-strapped wartime, United States establishes the bracero program to allow temporary foreign laborers.
1943	The Chinese Exclusion law is repealed.
1948	The Displaced Persons Act allows 400,000 refugees to enter America.
1952	Overriding President Truman's veto, Congress passes the Walter-McCarran Act: it reaffirms the national origins quota, sets preferences for skilled workers and relatives of U.S. citizens, increases screening of immigrants, and established the Asia-Pacific Triangle Quota of 2,000 immigrants per year from Asia.
1964	Bracero Program is repealed.
1965	Immigration and Nationality Act of 1965 is passed. It abolishes the national origins quota system, and makes family-reunification the cornerstone of American immigration policy. For the first time, a numerical ceiling of 120,000 is set for the Western Hemisphere (and 170,000 for the rest of the world with a 20,000 per-country limit).
1976	The Immigration and Nationality Act amendments of 1976 places 20,000 per-country limit to the Western hemisphere—the first time in U.S. history.
1978	Congress established the Select Commission on Immigration and Refugee Policy to investigate policy options.
1980	The Refugee Act expands the definition of a refugee to allow anyone fleeing political persecution to qualify as a refugee.
1986	The Immigration Reform and Control Act of 1986 tries to curb illegal immigration: it grants amnesty to million of illegal aliens and places employer sanctions.
1990	The Immigration Act of 1990 increases annual immigration by forty-percent: slots for employment-based immigrants increase, and a special "independent" country provision allow increased immigration from nations adversely affected by the 1965 act.
1994	The U.S. Commission on Immigration Reform recommends curtailing legal immigration.
1996	Congress considers a bill that would reduce legal immigration by a third, but the bill founders. Congress instead appropriates funds to beef up border control to fend off illegal immigration.

Source: U.S. Select Commission on Immigration and Refugee Policy (SCIRP). *U.S. Immigration Policy and the National Interest: The Final Report* (1981), pp. 88–89, and various *New York Times* articles.

"land of opportunity." In short, Americans of all races, creeds, and origins have at one time or another opposed immigration.

Anti-immigration fervor has steadily increased in the past three decades, yet no major restrictionist policies have been enacted during this time period. This leads us to the puzzling question: Why do restrictionists today, in comparison to their predecessors, have so much trouble enacting their agenda? Before jumping into this question, a quick review of America's immigration policy is in order.

THE OPEN-DOOR POLICY AND THE HAMILTON-JEFFERSON DEBATE (1700s–1880s)

Throughout much of the eighteenth century, the British crown encouraged immigration to America to create a market for its exports and expand its empire.[4] The government even provided free transportation for some people to move to America and established a simple naturalization process for non-English citizens. The initial colonists, in turn, did their best to attract more of their brethren to the New World. William Penn, for example, sojourned to Germany to bring immigrants to Pennsylvania.[5] Some immigrants were lured to help build cities in the sparsely populated New World, while others were brought in to help fend off Indians, who frequently clashed with the European settlers. Without any laws limiting immigration and a promise of religious and economic freedom, the colonial population burgeoned. The inhabitants of the original Thirteen Colonies were primarily of British stock, although there were some blacks and Indians intermixed with the European colonists. Even then, the American colonists already showed a nativist streak. They directed their animus mainly against Catholics, who were often considered agents of France and Spain, then the main enemies of the British empire. It was not surprising to have non-British immigrants socially, if not legally, ostracized.[6] Esteemed colonists like Benjamin Franklin espoused nativist views and derided German immigrants as "boors."

Notwithstanding this xenophobic streak among the colonists, the laissez-faire policy toward immigration continued after the American colonists asserted their independence from Britain. In fact, throughout the 1800s, immigration to America increased dramatically. During the 1820s, 150,000 immigrants entered the United States. By the 1840s, an additional 2,100,000 people had immigrated, and in the 1850s alone, nearly 2,500,000 immigrants came to America. One out of every seven Americans was either an immigrant or a child of an immigrant by 1860.[7] As the number of immigrants increased, their ethnic stock changed. From 1820 to 1860, 95% of all immigrants came from Northern and Western Europe.[8] From 1861 to 1900, that percentage dropped to 68, and by 1930, nearly seven out of ten immigrants were from Southern and Eastern Europe. The first large wave of immigration in the nineteenth century occurred from 1845 to 1854 when the Irish, fleeing the potato famine, and the Germans, many of whom wanted to escape the political turmoil of Europe, came in droves.[9] The second wave, which included a more ethnically diverse lot (such as Scandinavians and Chinese), occurred from 1865 to 1875.

A rapidly growing nation requires a huge influx of labor, so America not surprisingly had a virtually open-door policy. The federal government did not enact any substantive restrictionist law until 1882 and only started to count the number of immigrants in 1819.[10] There was no bureaucracy to handle immigration policy because international migration did not become a major issue for most nations until well into the nineteenth century.[11] The United States Constitution, for example, makes no mention of immigration except for brief references to the ban of slave importation until 1808 and the Congress's right to "establish a uniform rule of naturalization."[12]

The lack of any federal policy did not mean that the issue of immigration was ignored. Quite the contrary—the Hamiltonians and the Jeffersonians sparred over differing conceptions of citizenship.[13] Like so many other seminal political questions, the issue over immigration had its genesis in the debate between Hamilton's nationalist conservatism and Jefferson's universal liberalism.

A man of paradoxes, Thomas Jefferson appears sometimes to be an inscrutable historical figure. His actions often did not reflect his beliefs—take slavery for example. This man who professed that all men were created equal and thundered against the immorality of slavery also owned dozens of slaves. Jefferson can appear equally confusing on immigration. In his *Notes on the State of Virginia*, he had less than charitable words for immigrants, impugning them as intemperate. But there was a different side, too. Jefferson paid homage to immigrants by suggesting that a West Indian painter's schema of a six-field shield, each one representing one of the six largest immigrant groups to the British colonies, be the Great Seal of the United States.[14] Jefferson also had a politically expedient reason for his proimmigration view: immigrants, shunned by the aristocratic and nativist Federalists, felt more comfortable in Jefferson's Republican party. And it should be remembered that Jefferson, in the Declaration of Independence, excoriated King George III because, "He has endeavoured to prevent the Population of these States; for that Purpose obstructing the Laws of Naturalization of Foreigners; refusing to pass others to encourage their Migrations hither."

Most important, the classical liberal notions of "life, liberty and the pursuit of happiness" expounded in the Declaration of Independence articulated the concept of citizenship in terms of abstract, universal ideas. What mattered was not so much ethnicity or religion but rather adherence to universal ideas of democracy, liberty, and freedom. Anyone who subscribed to these beliefs could be an American. It is noteworthy to mention that Jefferson thought that Indians, who were widely regarded as incorrigible savages by most Europeans, could be assimilated into the new America.[15] Though Virginia law at the time prohibited miscegenation with both blacks and Indians, Jefferson, as President, told a group of Indians on December 21, 1808, "You will mix with us by marriage, your blood will run in our veins, and will spread with us over this great island."[16] This sentiment colored his view on the assimilability of immigrants. Though he may have not always practiced what he preached, "Jefferson sought to open up American politics to a better fulfillment of the goals and values he set forth in the Declaration of Independence. Equality, in both opportunity and in political freedom and expression, became the guide for American democracy," according to one historian.[17] In short, Jefferson established the regnant "liberal tradition" (as coined by historian Louis Hartz) in America that set the intellectual foundation for a liberal and open immigration policy.[18]

Jefferson's political nemesis, Alexander Hamilton, despite being an immigrant from the West Indies, was wary of immigration.[19] "Foreigners will generally be apt to bring with them attachments to the persons they have left behind; to the country of their nativity, and to particular customs and manners," said Hamilton in 1802. He continued: "The influx of foreigners must, therefore, tend to produce a heterogeneous compound; to change and corrupt the national spirit. . . . The United States have already felt the evils of incorporating a large number of foreigners into their national mass; by promoting in different classes different predilections in favor of particular foreign nations, and antipathies against others, it has served very much to divide the community and to distract our councils."[20]

This view was shared by most Federalists, who represented, as one historian put it, the "nativist party."[21] Their aversion toward foreigners was most evident in the passage of the Alien Act, probably the first law designed to regulate immigrants. The act lengthened the naturalization residency requirement from five to fourteen years, and allowed the deportation of "dangerous" aliens. The Alien Act, along with the Sedition Act, is of course, most known for the reaction it spawned: the Virginia and Kentucky Resolutions by Thomas Jefferson and James Madison. What is less emphasized in history books is that the Alien Act represented the Federalists' vain attempt to hold on to power by disenfranchising immigrants who voted overwhelmingly for Thomas Jefferson's Republican Party and to punish the political enemies of the Federalists.[22]

The laws, however, reflected more than just a xenophobic power grab; they represented a genuine fear that the customs and the culture brought by foreigners would upset American society. The Federalist Party was the first national "conservative" political party, and it wanted to conserve the traditions of America.[23] As Russell Kirk, one of the more erudite scholars of American conservatism, explains, "the conservative adheres to custom, convention and continuity. It is old custom that enables to live together peaceably; the destroyers of custom demolish more than they know or desire."[24] Thus, conservatives have disdain for abstraction (as expounded by Jeffersonians) and instead, prefer custom as their guide. Consequently, the Federalists dreaded the prospect of French radicals foisting their abstract idea of egalitarianism on America. In an address to the Electors of the State of New York, Hamilton warned that the Jeffersonians "have openly avowed their attachment to the excessive principles of the French revolution. . . . In regard to these sects, which compose the pith and essence of the antifederal party, we believe it to be true, that the contest between the tyranny of jacobinism, which confounds and levels every thing, and the mild reign of liberty."[25] Citizenship had roots in custom, culture, and (British) ethnicity, according to Hamilton.

The politics of immigration today owe much to the debate between Thomas Jefferson and Alexander Hamilton. Many contemporary liberals and neoconservative internationalists hark back to the Jeffersonian universal ideals as the basis of American citizenship. Mark Falcoff, a scholar at the neoconservative American Enterprise Institute, for example, echoed shades of Jefferson when he recently wrote that, "Uniquely among nations, America is a 'proposition country'; it has not history and identity apart from certain eighteenth-century political notions embodied in its Constitution and Common Law."[26] And political pundit Ben Wattenberg, a former speechwriter for Lyndon Johnson, in a book about immigration heralded America as the "first universal nation."[27] On the other side, social conservatives today stress Hamilton's cultural and ethnic concepts of citizenship (such as when Pat Buchanan said, in his trademark inflammatory style, that he would prefer a thousand English immigrants over a thousand Zulus). The American public has sympathy for both arguments, which explains its ambivalence on this issue.

THE DOOR-AJAR PERIOD (1880–1920)

The trend from the previous decades—increased immigration from non-Western and non–Northern European states—continued into the twentieth century. Italians, Russian Jews, and other Slavs came in larger numbers. The American Jewish population surged from 250,000 in 1877 to over 4 million in 1927.[28] Total immigration numbers exploded as well. Over one million immigrants entered annually in 1905, 1906, 1907, 1910, 1913, and 1914.[29] The sheer level of immigration meant that its impact was widely felt, making it an important issue. Both restrictionists and immigrationists began proffering their arguments, many of which sound very familiar today.

One major point of contention was the economic impact of immigrants. Business interests actively supported immigration as a cheap source of labor; railroads, in particular, depended on immigrants to toil on the back-breaking work of laying the rails. Many organs of the popular press echoed the theme that immigrants were an economic boon to America. In the April 1882 issue of the *North American Review*, a writer precisely claimed that each immigrant had "in his brain and muscle a power equal to a capital of $51,000."[30] The *Saturday Evening Post* opined that, "a million healthy immigrants, quite uneducated, are capable of adding and probably would add a hundred million dollars a year to the wealth of our country."[31]

At the same time though, many Americans feared that immigrants would depress wages and displace native-born Americans. The establishment of national labor unions (such as the Federation of Organized Trades and Labor Unions in 1881 and the American Federation of Labor in 1886) gave a stronger voice to restrictionism.[32] As one *North American Review* article argued, "Far more valuable than sudden wealth [that immigrants may bring] is the maintenance of good wages among American working men and the exclusion of an unlimited supply of low-class labor with which they cannot compete."[33] These arguments, both pro and con, probably could be published in today's *Wall Street Journal* op-ed page or an AFL-CIO newsletter, and few would realize that they were uttered over a century ago.

Labor unions and other restrictionists (such as state and local governments that had to bear the costs of immigration) relied on more than just economic arguments. They repeatedly used racialistic appeals to impugn the character of the new immigrants from Southern and Eastern Europe and Asia. This first started as an attack against the moral character of the newer immigrants, and it eventually was transformed into the pseudoscientific language of eugenics: immigrants lacked the intellectual capacity to enjoy self-government in our republic.[34] In a popular nineteenth-century book by Baynard Taylor, the Chinese were described as "morally, the most debased people on the face of earth."[35] A congressional hearing held in 1880 concurred: "As the safety of republican institutions requires that the franchise shall be only by those who have a love and appreciation for our institutions, and this rule excludes the great mass of the Chinese from the ballot as a necessary means of public safety, yet the application of the rule deprives them of the only adequate protection which can exist in a republic for the security of any distinct, large class of persons."[36]

Southern and Eastern Europeans received no better treatment. In a 1910 article in the *North American Review*, Robert De C. Ward flatly asserted, "Immigrants from most of the world except Britain and Northern Europe are inferior. They threaten our vitality and our national intelligence."[37] Or take *Atlantic Monthly*'s jeremiad: "The entrance into our political, social and industrial life of such vast masses of peasantry, degraded below our utmost conceptions, is a matter which no intelligent patriot can look upon without gravest apprehension and alarm. . . . They are beaten men from beaten races; representing the worst failures in the struggle for existence."[38] Not only were Southern and Eastern Europeans too morally and intellectually feeble to enjoy republican institutions, they could not even assimilate into the American culture. As the *Literary Digest* put it, "Our boasted power of Yankeefying all the races that come hither is doing them and us more harm than good."[39]

All this pressure for restrictionism did not immediately translate into a policy change because the federal government had no institutions or bureaucracies to handle immigration. As one political scientist noted, "There was no national policy network for immigration policy at the beginning of this era. There were no congressional committees to make immigration policy, no national administrative agencies to regulate immigration, and no nationally organized interest groups to advocate changes in the nation's immigration laws."[40] Prior to the turn of the century, individual states had regulated immigration. As early as the 1820s, a handful of states had enacted laws preventing paupers from entering.[41] Other methods of regulating immigration included levying taxes on immigrants and imposing additional qualifications. But in the mid-nineteenth century, federal courts began nullifying state laws regulating immigration on the grounds that the federal government had sole power in areas of national sovereignty and regulation of commerce.[42] States faced a quandary posed by the uniquely American system of federalism: they had to bear the social and fiscal costs of immigration—which included an additional burden on public charity programs as well as public disorder caused by riots against immigrants—but they could not regulate it.[43] States began pressuring the federal government to address this problem, with New York, Minnesota, and California all petitioning Congress to restrict immigration.[44]

The federal government was at first unwilling to intervene in these matters. First, the federal government, as mentioned before, had no national policy network, state bureaucracy, or administrative agency to handle immigration. Second, the chief executive feared that racially based restrictions would sour relations with other countries. President Rutherford B. Hayes, for example, vetoed the anti-Chinese Fifteen Passengers bill because it would have contravened the Burlingame treaty, which allowed the free movement of people between the United States and China.[45] This foreign policy imperative would reappear in later years: Congress, heeding the demands of its local constituents, would push for restrictions, while the president, thinking of national foreign policy demands, would fight limitations on immigration.

By the 1880s, Congress finally felt compelled to establish some restrictions. With anti-Chinese feelings hitting a high-fever pitch and anti-immigrant riots breaking out in many cities, Congress voted for the Chinese Exclusion Act of 1882, preventing immigration from China for ten years. President Chester A. Arthur vetoed it, but he later signed another version of the bill because the State Department rationalized that it was better foreign policy to abrogate a treaty than to anger China by allowing its nationals to be killed by westerners.[46]

Then Congress passed the Act of 1882, which prevented convicts, lunatics, idiots, and those likely to become public charges from entering. Under pressure from the newly formed national labor unions, Congress then went to task on the Contract Labor Laws of 1885 and 1887, barring the much detested contract laborers, who were thought to depress wages of native-born Americans.

Although these laws did not curtail immigration dramatically and served mainly a symbolic role, they were important in that they nationalized the issue of immigration. It was now a federal, not a state, issue. National institutions and bureaucracies were soon created once immigration became a responsibility of the federal government. In 1888, the House established the Ford Commission to study the immigration problem further. By 1893, both the House and the Senate had formed permanent standing committees on immigration.[47] These committees became points of access for nascent interest groups. National labor unions, for instance, sprouted in the late nineteenth century and were a potent restrictionist force to counteract business interest groups that wanted a liberal immigration policy.

Administrative agencies were then rapidly developed. Following the recommendations of the Ford Commission, Congress created a Bureau of Immigration in the Treasury Department in 1891. The bureau was headed by a commissioner general of immigration, who, over the years, gradually gained more administrative power to regulate contract labor and oversee the Chinese exclusion acts.[48] At the same time that the bureau was established, Congress also founded an immigrant receiving facility at Ellis Island in New York. Then, after the 1890 census reported problems associated with immigration, a Division of Naturalization was created under the Department of Labor better to monitor immigrants.

The building-up of national administrative structures continued into the twentieth century. In 1905, Theodore Roosevelt formed a presidential commission to study immigration, which recommended the creation of a unified Bureau of Immigration and Naturalization.[49] Two years later, Congress convened a joint commission to study immigration once again. Better known as the Dillingham Commission (named after Senator William P. Dillingham), it released a voluminous study that asserted the moral and intellectual inferiority of recent immigrants like the Jews and Italians. Heavily swayed by then-popular eugenics theories, the commission recommended curtailing the number of "subpar" immigrants through literacy tests. Such thought had gained credence among the public. A 1915 *North American Review* article confidently declared that, "It is indisputable that immigrants from the North Western countries are decidedly preferable to those from South Eastern. Their morals are better, their average of literacy and of general intelligence are far higher, their physical condition is better and their civic usefulness is superior."[50]

The Dillingham Commission's recommendations found their way into the restrictionist Immigration and Naturalization Act of 1917. After suffering three previous presidential vetoes of literacy tests, Congress was finally able to override President Woodrow Wilson's veto of the 1917 bill and codified a literacy test to limit Southern and Eastern Europeans. The law also excluded alcoholics, vagrants, the insane, women entering for immoral purposes, and anarchists.[51] Moreover, it virtually barred immigration from most of Asia. The 1917 act did not substantially stem the tide of immigrants, but it was salient for two reasons. First, it continued to develop national bureaucratic agencies and policy networks that dealt with immigration. Second, it foreboded the looming restrictionist legislation that would prevail until the Immigration and Nationality Act of 1965.

THE RESTRICTIONIST ERA (1921–1964)

The years leading to the 1920s were a tumultuous time for both America and the world. After suffering an economic recession, the country became embroiled in a devastating world war. After the war, a somber isolationist mood prevailed. As the fear of foreign radicals corrupting the "pristine" American way of life grew, so did feelings of nationalism and "Americanism." Eugenics theory was also still in vogue, further fueling nativist sentiment. "The immigrant seldom brings in his intellectual baggage anything of use to us . . . the admission into our electorate of backward men—men whose mental, moral and physical standards are lower than our own—must inevitably retard our own social progress and thrust us behind the more uniformly civilized nations of the world," warned the *Atlantic Monthly*.[52] Many Americans were especially afraid that the economic turmoil in Europe would start a mass migration to the United States.

Under this cloud of fear, Congress quickly acted to shut the doors of immigration. In 1920, the House voted to end immigration altogether, although the Senate dissented.[53] Then in 1921, pushed by groups ranging from the American Federation of Labor to the Immigration Restrictionist League, Congress passed the first national origins quota bill.[54] Under the bill, each nation was given a quota of 3% of the foreign-born population in the United States at the 1910 census for a total annual quota of around 360,000 (no quotas were allotted to Asian countries because most of them were already barred by the 1917 act). By setting 1910 as the baseline year, the law limited the number of Southern and Eastern Europeans as most immigrants in 1910 had come from Northern and Western Europe. Because this law was intended to curtail European immigration, it did not place any quotas on the Western Hemisphere: Mexicans and Canadians were free to migrate to the United States without any numerical limits.

The quotas set by the 1921 act were only temporary and expired in 1924. As Congress began deliberating immigration policy in 1924, business groups like the National Association of Manufacturers and the U.S. Chamber of Commerce lobbied to ease the quotas. The president of U.S. Steel denounced the 1921 act as "one of the worst things this country has ever done for itself economically."[55] But the economic arguments of business were no match for the fear of job displacement and the eugenics thought pervading Congress. "The hour has come. It may be even now too late for the white race in America, the English-speaking people, the laborer of high ideals, to assert his superiority in the work of civilization and to save America from the menace of further immigration of undesirable aliens," averred one congressman from Maine.[56]

Congress passed the Immigration Act of 1924, setting in place an even stricter quota system. The census base year was shifted from 1910 to 1890, assuring that even fewer Southern and Eastern Europeans would enter. The total quota was reduced as well, from 360,000 to 165,000.

It should be noted that the 1924 law still did not impose any quotas on Mexico. In fact, it would not be until 1969 that the United States would set per-country limits on the Western Hemisphere. This is not because Americans saw Mexicans as their equals—quite the contrary. Rather, there were few forces—interest groups or state bureaucracies— that were overly concerned with limiting immigration from Mexico because the levels were low. From 1890 to 1950, only 811,000 Mexicans legally immigrated to the United States, despite the fact that there were no quotas or limits on Mexico. Contrast that number with the over 19 million people who immigrated from Europe during the same time period.[57] Furthermore, the western United States was still relatively sparsely populated during the early twentieth century—unlike

the Eastern urban areas teeming with immigrants—and so there was
no major sense of exigency to place ceilings. Naturally, most of the
attention was focused on European immigration.

The end of World War II placed more stress on American immigration policy. Millions of people fleeing the turmoil of postwar Europe
wanted to come to the United States, but America's inflexible and
restrictive quota system would not allow it. Ethnic groups, along with
the State Department—which wanted to delay the establishment of a
Jewish state in Palestine—pushed Congress to accept refugees outside
of the annual quotas.[58] Although America had historically served as a
haven for political refugees, it never had a special legal category for
"refugees." Despite some legislators balking at the idea, Congress
nevertheless passed the Displaced Persons Act of 1948, setting a legal
precedent for a special category of refugees outside of the normal
immigration policy.

The next substantial immigration law, the McCarran-Walter Act of
1952, showed that American immigration policy was at a crossroads.
Although some historians treat it as an essentially restrictive legislation,
the reality is more complex. The act represented an amalgamation of
foreign *and* domestic policy interests as well as restrictive *and* liberalizing provisions. Views on race and on America's role in the world were
changing, and so was the country's immigration policy.

Passed by an override of President Truman's veto, the act reaffirmed
the national origins quota system first established in 1921. Within each
country's quota, there was a broad preference system of visas allocated
on the basis of job skills (50% of the visas) and family kinship (the other
50%). Security concerns of communist subversion played a large role
in casting the restrictive mold of the 1952 act. Many people feared that
communist foreigners would infiltrate the United States through lax
immigration policies. After all, it was a time when the Soviet Union had
gobbled up much of Eastern Europe and blockaded Europe; when
China and quite possibly Korea were "lost" to the communists; and
when seemingly impeccable people like Alger Hiss were implicated in
espionage.

Overtly racist arguments, however, were on the wane. The political
rhetoric of the nation had changed. It was becoming politically unac-
ceptable openly to espouse ethnocentric or racist views. Congress,
despite maintaining the racially biased national origins quota, denied
any racial motivation. The trend toward deracialization was set in
motion earlier when Congress, in a symbolic display of racial goodwill

and liberalism, repealed the Chinese Exclusion Act and the racial ban on citizenship (although the maintenance of the national quotas and the establishment of an Asian-Pacific Triangle quota of 2,000 in the 1952 act meant that, in reality, very few Asians could immigrate).

It was not just liberalized views on race that were responsible for these actions; foreign policy had some role as well. In the fight against communism, America did not want gratuitously to insult Asian nations by maintaining race-specific bars on Asians when national quotas would be sufficient to limit them. The 1952 act also continued to exempt the Western hemisphere from numerical ceilings in order to maintain its Good Neighbor Policy with Central America. Despite these liberal accommodations, Truman still saw the restrictive quota system as an impediment to foreign policy. In vetoing the bill, he said:

> The countries of Eastern Europe have fallen under the Communist yoke—they are silenced, fenced off by barbed wire and minefields—no one passes their borders but at the risk of his life. We do not need to be protected against immigrants from these countries—on the contrary we want to stretch out a helping hand, to save those who have managed to flee into Western Europe, to succor those who are brave enough to escape from barbarism, to welcome and restore them against the day when their countries will, as we hope, be free again. These are only a few examples of the absurdity, the cruelty of carrying over into this year of 1952 the isolationist limitations of our 1924 law.[59]

The four decades from 1921 to 1964 saw dramatic policy changes. The symbolic laws from the previous decades finally led to draconian restrictionist laws that virtually halted immigration. During the period of the Great Depression and World War II, only a few thousand immigrants entered America each year. Yet by the end of World War II, America had unquestionably become the global superpower. America became consumed by foreign policy considerations during the Cold War era, and in the fight against the threat of international communism, it could not afford needlessly to offend other nations by continuing ethnically biased immigration policies. Furthermore, pressure mounted to allow in the millions of refugees fleeing communist despotism. Either America's immigration policy or its foreign policy would have to change. And it was the immigration laws that dramatically changed in the coming decades.

THE DUTCH DOOR ERA (1965–PRESENT)

The McCarran-Walter Act proved to be a woefully inadequate immigration policy. From 1952 to 1965, only 61% of the allowable quota visas was issued—although thousands of people waited to immigrate to the United States—because many of these people were from the "wrong" country.[60] Great Britain, for example, had a large bulk of the national origins quota, but much of its allotment went unused, while there was a huge backlog in other countries with small quotas. The United States ended up circumventing the stringent national origins quota in many cases by, for example, using the parole power to accept refugees. In all, only one out of every three immigrants admitted during this period came through the national origins quota system. It was an irrational policy, and pressure mounted to overhaul the system.

Another impetus for reform came from the civil rights movement. As American society became more racially tolerant and as protests raised the conscience of the nation, racially biased policies were abolished and civil rights laws were enacted. This zeitgeist spread to immigration policy. The discriminatory effect of the national origins quota and the Asia-Pacific Triangle was seen as a moral blight on America. Indeed, it was a sign of the times that the country—which originally had restricted immigration in order to limit the number of Catholics—elected for the first time, a Catholic, John F. Kennedy, as president in 1960. Kennedy, who had earlier written a pro-immigration tract called *A Nation of Immigrants*, proposed a major overhaul of immigration policy. His proposal called for the gradual removal of the national origins quota and the Asia-Pacific Triangle, though it maintained a cap on non-Western nations at 165,000. It also recommended allotting one-half of the visas to people with special skills or education and the other half to close relatives of people already here—the same ratio as set in the McCarran-Walter Act.[61]

Kennedy's untimely death delayed immigration reform temporarily until Lyndon Johnson, who had already initiated his ambitious Great Society, decided to take up the issue. Johnson's rout of Goldwater in 1964 helped give him a liberal Congress receptive to such a reform. And the vibrant economy of the 1960s, with its rapid growth and low unemployment, meant that even the usual opponents of immigration (like organized labor) were supportive or did not put up much of a fight. The bill passed easily in both the House and the Senate and was signed by Johnson in 1965.

Johnson's version of the bill was more generous than Kennedy's. The Immigration Act of 1965, which set the basic framework for the next thirty years, abolished both the national origins quota and the Asia-Pacific Triangle and, instead, instituted a seven-level preference system. The first level of preference was for unmarried sons and daughters of U.S. citizens; the second preference was for spouses and unmarried children of permanent residents; third, for scientists and artists of exceptional ability; fourth, for married sons and daughters of U.S. citizens; fifth, for brothers and sisters of U.S. citizens; sixth, for skilled and unskilled workers in short supply; and seventh, for refugees. A whopping 74% of the visas was to be issued on the basis of family reunification, while skill-based visas comprised only 20% of the total. The other 6% was allocated for refugees. The act also established a worldwide cap of 290,000: 120,000 for Western Hemisphere countries and 170,000 for non-Western. The cap on Western Hemisphere nations—the first time that such a ceiling was set—was put in place partly because of restrictionists' fear that increasing population in Latin America would flood America in the future. This decision—along with the termination of the temporary guest-worker program in 1964— would have major unintended and unforeseen repercussions for American immigration policy in the future. There was also a 20,000 per-country cap on non–Western Hemisphere nations but none for Western Hemisphere countries until amendments to the law added one in 1976.[62] The world-wide cap of 290,000, however, was almost meaningless. Immediate family members of U.S. citizens (i.e., spouses, parents, and minor children) were and continue to be exempted from these caps. Thus, annual immigration would often exceed the cap.

The Immigration Act of 1965 had many other unintended consequences. Senator Edward Kennedy, the main sponsor of the bill, claimed that it "would not inundate America with immigrants from any one country or area or the most populated and economically deprived nations of Africa and Asia."[63] And Attorney General Robert Kennedy predicted that the abolition of the Asia-Pacific Triangle would mean that "5,000 immigrants [from Asia] could come in the first year, but we do not expect that there would be any great influx after that."[64] In fact, many of the supporters of the national origins quota system defended this bill as a way to reaffirm the patterns of the old system. "But Asiatics having far fewer immediate family members now in the United States than Southern Europeans, will automatically arrive in far fewer numbers than Italians, Greeks and other southern European stock. Yet, there is no sting in the new law to offend Asian nations. Asians will qualify on the same basis as others, though far fewer will be able to do so," claimed a magazine of the American Legion, a traditional opponent of increased immigration.[65] When Lyndon Johnson signed the bill in front of the Statue of Liberty, he averred, "This is not a revolutionary bill. It does not affect the lives of millions. It will not reshape the structure of our daily lives."[66]

Yet the bill was revolutionary. It initiated a massive change in the ethnic makeup of the immigrants—from primarily European to mostly Third World. Before its passage, most immigrants came from Europe. Today, about 80% of the immigrants come from either Asia or Latin America. Within ten years of the bill's passage, Asian immigration had increased six-fold.[67] Certain Third World countries benefited tremendously. In the ten years after the 1965 act's passage, immigration from India increased 3,000%; from Korea, 1,328%; Philippines, 1,200%; while immigration from the United Kingdom declined by 120%; from Austria, 767%; Ireland, 77%.[68] How did this happen? There were many "push" factors, such as economic or political turmoil that led people in the Third World to come to America. But there were "pull" factors as well: the family reunification criterion unintentionally started a phenomenon called "chain migration," which occurs when one immigrant applies to bring his family members, who then apply to bring their family members, and so on. The fifth preference level—for brothers and sisters of citizens—was used the most in this "chain migration."

The 1965 Immigration Act also increased the numerical level of immigration, from less than 300,000 in 1964 to nearly a million each year during the 1980s. These developments made many Americans uneasy, and public opinion polls reflected the growing opposition to the current policy. The legislation also had another major unintended consequence: it dramatically increased *illegal* immigration, which completely altered the framework of immigration politics and severely hampered legal immigration reform. That momentous development will be discussed in the next chapter.

NOTES

1. United States Select Commission on Immigration and Refugee Policy (SCIRP), *U.S. Immigration Policy and the National Interest: The Final Report and Recommendations of the Select Commission on Immigration and Refugee Policy with Supplemental Views by Commissioners* (Washington, D.C.: U.S. Government Printing Office, 1981), p. 88.

2. Ibid., p. 2.

3. Michael C. LeMay, "U.S. Immigration Policy and Politics," LeMay, ed., *The Gatekeepers: Comparative Immigration Policy* (New York: Praeger, 1989), p. 2. These four era names are adopted roughly from LeMay's chapter.

4. Maxine S. Seller, "Historical Perspectives on American Immigration Policy: Case Studies and Current Implications," Richard R. Hofstetter, ed., *U.S. Immigration Policy* (Durham, N.C.: Duke Press Policy Studies, 1984), p. 140.

5. Ibid., p. 140.

6. Chilton Williamson, Jr., *The Immigration Mystique: America's False Conscience* (New York: Basic Books, 1996), pp. 25–26.

7. Seller, "Historical Perspectives," p. 144.

8. SCIRP, *Final Report*, p. 94.

9. Michael C. LeMay, *From Open Door to Dutch Door: An Analysis of U.S. Immigration Policy since 1820* (New York: Praeger, 1987), pp. 21–30.

10. Tina A. Campbell, "Immigration Law: The Role of the Supreme Court in Policy Development," *New England Law Review* 22 (1987): 135.

11. Ibid., p. 135.

12. United States Constitution, Article I, Section 8.

13. For a brief discussion on the Federalists' and the Republicans' views on immigration, see Williamson, *The Immigration Mystique*, pp. 23–35.

14. Williamson, p. 27.

15. Fawn M. Brodie, *Thomas Jefferson: An Intimate History* (New York: W. W. Norton & Company, 1974), p. 434.

16. Ibid., p. 434.

17. Patrick M. Garry, *Liberalism and American Identity* (Kent, Ohio: Kent State University Press, 1992), p. 55.

18. Louis Hartz, *The Liberal Tradition in America* (San Diego: Harcourt Brace Jovanovich, 1955).

19. Ironically, restrictionists often are immigrants themselves. Peter Brimelow, a senior editor at *Forbes* and the leading anti-immigrant voice in America today, was born in Canada.

20. As quoted in Peter Brimelow, *Alien Nation: Common Sense about America's Immigration Disaster* (New York: Random House, 1995), p. 191.

21. Wilfred E. Binkley, *American Political Parties: Their Natural History* (New York: Alfred A. Knopf, 1945), p. 80.

22. Robert G. McCloskey and Sanford Levinson, *The American Supreme Court*, 2d ed. (Chicago: The University of Chicago Press, 1994), p. 23.

23. The term "conservative" here is used in the traditional, Burkean sense of prescription and conservation. I am not referring to today's "conservatives" (or more appropriately, libertarians), who are really nineteenth century liberals.

24. Russell Kirk, *The Politics of Prudence* (Bryn Mawr, Penn.: Intercollegiate Studies Institute, 1993), p. 18.

25. Morton Frisch, ed., *The Selected Writings and Speeches of Alexander Hamilton* (Washington, D.C.: The American Enterprise Institute, 1985), pp. 465–78.

26. As quoted in Williamson, *Immigration Mystique*, p. 112.

27. Ben J. Wattenberg, *The First Universal Nation: Leading Indicators and Ideas about the Surge of America in the 1990s* (New York: The Free Press, 1991).

28. LeMay, *Open Door*, p. 38.

29. Seller, "Historical Perspective," p. 148.

30. Rita J. Simon and Susan H. Alexander, *The Ambivalent Welcome: Print Media, Public Opinion and Immigration* (New York: Praeger, 1993), p. 51.

31. Ibid., p. 67.

32. Keith Fitzgerald, *The Face of the Nation: Immigration, the State and the National Identity* (Stanford, Calif.: Stanford University Press, 1996), p. 106.

33. Simon and Alexander, *Ambivalent Welcome*, p. 53.

34. Fitzgerald, *Face of the Nation*, pp. 116–17.

35. Ibid., p. 120.

36. As quoted in ibid., p. 121.

37. Simon and Alexander, *Ambivalent Welcome*, p. 59.

38. Ibid., p. 128.

39. Ibid., p. 94.

40. Fitzgerald, *Face of the Nation*, p. 106. Much of the following information on the national institutions and bureaucracies on immigration is based on Fitzgerald's helpful chapter, "The Development and Expansion of a Sectoral State."

41. Williamson, *Immigration Mystique*, p. 33.

42. Fitzgerald, *Face of the Nation*, p. 110.

43. This system of federalism plagues states like California and Florida today, especially on the issue of illegal immigration. The use of social services places disproportionate stress on these high impact states, but only the federal government can regulate immigration. Proposition 187, which was passed overwhelmingly by California voters in 1994 to deny social services to illegal immigrants, faces legal obstacles because the courts see it as an attempt by a state to usurp a federal function.

44. Fitzgerald, *Face of the Nation*, pp. 104–5.

45. Ibid., p. 112.

46. Ibid., p. 114.

47. Ibid., p. 116.

48. Ibid., p. 126.

49. Ibid., p. 127.

50. Simon and Alexander, *Ambivalent Welcome*, p. 58.

51. Fitzgerald, *Face of the Nation*, p. 128.

52. Simon and Alexander, *Ambivalent Welcome*, p. 131.

53. LeMay, *Open Door*, p. 77.

54. Ibid., p. 81.

55. John Higham, *Strangers in the Land: Patterns of American Nativism: 1860–1925.* (New Brunswick, N.J.: Rutgers University Press, 1955), p. 315.

56. As quoted in LeMay, *Open Door*, p. 85.

57. U.S. Immigration and Naturalization Service, *Statistical Yearbook of the Immigration and Naturalization Service, 1994* (Washington, D.C.: U.S. Government Printing Office, 1996), p. 27.

58. Fitzgerald, *Face of the Nation*, pp. 195–97.

59. As quoted in Vernon M. Briggs, Jr., *Mass Immigration and the National Interest* (Armonk, N.Y.: M.E. Sharpe, Inc., 1992), p. 100.

60. Ibid., p.102.

61. David M. Reimers, *Still the Golden Door: The Third World Comes to America* (New York: Columbia University Press, 1992), p. 64. Also see Briggs, *Mass Immigration*, p. 107.

62. Briggs, *Mass Immigration*, p. 110.

63. Ibid., p. 75.

64. David M. Reimers, "Recent Immigration Policy: An Analysis," Barry R. Chiswick, ed., *The Gateway: U.S. Immigration Issues and Policies* (Washington, D.C.: American Enterprise Institute, 1982), p. 35.

65. Reimers, *Golden Door*, p. 73.

66. Reimers, "Recent Immigration Policy," p. 38.

67. Reimers, *Golden Door*, p. 82.

68. LeMay, *Open Door*, p. 114.

Chapter 4

How Illegal Immigration Dwarfed Legal Immigration

When Congress abolished the national origins quota system and enacted a more liberal immigration policy in 1965, it placed a 120,000 annual cap on Western Hemisphere immigration. The cap, which took effect on July 1, 1968, marked the first time that America had placed a ceiling on Western Hemisphere countries (non–Western Hemisphere countries already had a 170,000 total and a 20,000 per-country limit at the time). Congress had established this cap because many members feared that burgeoning population and political turmoil in Latin America would lead to an exodus to the United States. A Senate report concluded that "the final inclusion of the ceiling in the enacted bill was a necessary quid pro quo in exchange for the abolishment of the national origins quota system."[1] Then in 1976, an annual ceiling of 20,000 immigrants per country was extended to Western Hemisphere countries. This per-country cap was added as a matter of fairness and equity. Without it, Mexico had taken a lion's share of Western Hemisphere allotments. In 1974, for example, over 45,000 Mexicans (excluding immediate family members who are exempt from the caps) came to America.[2] One legislator complained that by "discriminating in favor of the Mexican immigration, we are also discriminating against other countries in the Western Hemisphere."[3]

Some congressmen voiced concern at the time that per-country limits would unleash a wave of illegal immigration. They were right:

the decision to set ceilings on Western Hemisphere states would have a momentous impact on both illegal and legal immigration policies. The caps virtually precluded Mexicans without job skills or family members already residing in the United States from coming to America. Furthermore, even those with family members in the United States had to compete against each other for the 20,000 annual visas. Not surprisingly, an interminable backlog accumulated, and many had to wait several years to receive a visa. For many Mexicans, entering the United States illegally through the porous border became enticing and, in many instances, proved to be the only realistic way to come to America.

Since the 1965 act was about "fairness," the legislation established the same numerical caps for all the countries. But that made little practical sense. Equal per-country caps might have been fair, but it was unrealistic in thinking that people from countries sharing a border with the United States would not just enter illegally if they were denied visas. For example, a Mexican (or a Canadian) who did not receive a visa always had the option of illegally crossing the border with relative ease, while someone from, say, Ghana, did not have that option. It would have made more sense to allot more visas to Canadians or Mexicans and limit visas for other countries. Both Presidents Ford and Carter realized the inflexibility of the caps, and they wanted to increase the annual limits for our neighboring countries. In signing the 1976 amendments, Ford promised that he would increase the ceiling for Mexico, saying that the United States had a very special and historic relationship with Mexico. But both Ford and Carter were busy with other, more pressing economic problems; these proposals were never given serious attention and were not enacted.

Pressure to immigrate illegally to the United States had already begun to simmer earlier when Congress ended the guest-worker Bracero program in 1964. From 1942 to 1964, the Bracero program had recruited over 4.6 million Mexicans to come temporarily to the United States to work as agricultural workers during the growing season.[4] Initiated at the behest of powerful agri-businesses, the Bracero program brought workers who performed back-breaking labor for several months and then returned to Mexico after the growing season ended. Bringing these temporary guest-workers had stemmed the pressure to immigrate illegally to the United States, according to a study commissioned by the Secretary of Labor in 1959.[5] But many interest groups opposed the program. Organized labor viewed it as a threat because many of the braceros were not paid the prevailing wage (despite rules requiring growers to do so), and were not able to join unions. Religious organizations opposed it because they felt that agri-businesses exploited the workers. Unsympathetic to growers, the Johnson administration let the program die in 1964. Growers, however, had become dependent on these temporary hired hands. Likewise, many Mexicans had come to rely on these jobs to support their families, and they continued to arrive, albeit illegally, to the United States during the growing season. Other Mexicans got the "taste" of America while they were here during the growing season and decided to move permanently to the United States. The Immigration and Naturalization Service (INS) reported in 1970 that, "Since the expiration of the Mexican Agriculture Act on December 31, 1964, the number of deportable aliens located has continued on an upward climb."[6]

These limitations on immigration, along with "push" factors—such as improved transportation and high unemployment in Mexico—spurred thousands of Mexicans to enter the United States illegally starting in the late 1970s. (It is important to note that, contrary to images portrayed by the media, not all illegal immigrants cross the border from Mexico; a substantial percentage come from other parts of the world, and about 40% become "illegal" by overstaying their visas. But as of October 1992, Mexicans represented nearly 40% of the estimated illegal immigrant population in the United States—more than three times the total of the second highest ethnic group, Salvadorans).[7] Although the INS does not keep an accurate track of the number of illegal aliens who enter the United States annually, it does have data on the number of aliens apprehended, most of whom are caught crossing the border. As figure 4.1 reveals, the number of illegal aliens apprehended surged during the 1970s.[8]

This was not the first time that the United States had experienced substantial illegal immigration, although the magnitude and the duration of the problem were probably unparalleled in the history of this country. Statistics on the number of illegal aliens apprehended were not collected before 1920, but there were an estimated 1.5 million aliens captured from 1920 to 1950, a relatively low number when compared to the nearly 12 million caught during the 1980s alone.[9] Illegal immigration was not considered an important issue earlier in the century because relatively few people illegally crossed the border and the West was not as densely populated as today. During the 1950s,

Figure 4.1
Illegal Aliens Apprehended (1952–1994)

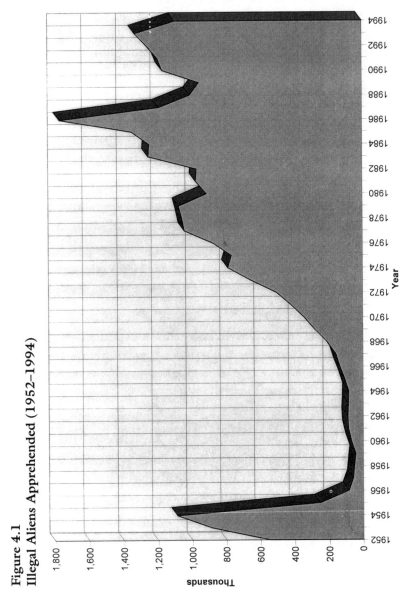

Source: Statistical Yearbook of the INS, 1994. (1996).

illegal immigration increased substantially, and the federal government responded by launching Operation Wetback, a military-style operation aimed at capturing and deporting undocumented workers. INS agents raided agricultural areas suspected of harboring illegal aliens, used roadblocks when needed, and ultimately deported over one million illegals.[10] The INS triumphantly reported in 1955 that, "The so-called 'wet-back' problem no longer exists. . . . The border has been secured."[11]

But the establishment of immigration ceilings in 1968 and 1976 limited the number of legal visas granted to Mexico, and illegal immigration began increasing again. The problem now was worse as hundreds of thousands of illegal aliens flowed into the United States each year. An Operation Wetback–style project was no longer possible by the 1970s because undocumented workers had diversified into other areas, such as light manufacturing, which made round-ups far more difficult. Moreover, increased consideration for civil liberties in the 1970s precluded such military-style operations.[12]

AGENDA-SETTING THEORIES AND IMMIGRATION

Each session, members of Congress introduce thousands of bills, but only a small handful ever receive any serious attention. How an issue attains prominence on the policy agenda of legislators has been the source of many scholarly studies. Political scientist Roger Cobb has postulated that there are two types of policy agenda: a public agenda, which "consists of issues which have achieved a high level of public interest and visibility," and the formal agenda, which "is the list of items which decision makers have formally accepted for serious consideration."[13] Some issues may pique the interest of the public but never make it to the formal agenda. Many never even make it to the public agenda.

How an issue piques the public's interest and becomes a part of the policymakers' formal agenda partly depends on the level of attention it receives from the public, interest groups, and the media. In a noted 1972 article in *The Public Interest*, Anthony Downs hypothesized that most issues undergo an "issue-attention cycle." He argued that a problem "suddenly leaps into prominence, remains there for a short time, and then—though still largely unresolved—gradually fades from the center of public attention."[14] The issue-attention cycle can be divided into five separate stages. In the first preproblem stage, an undesirable problem is bubbling but has not yet attracted public attention. Then, in the second stage, there is a sudden awareness and alarm over the problem. People put pressure on policymakers to take action. They believe that any problem is eminently solvable without any significant costs and fundamental changes. In the third stage, the public slowly realizes that some groups or individuals benefit from the maintenance of the status quo and that it is very costly to solve this problem. Soon there is a decline in interest—in the fourth stage—as the public gets bored by the issue or realizes the costs of the solution. In the final postproblem stage, the problem fades away from the public attention, but new programs or institutions that may have been created during this issue-attention cycle may persist.

This issue-attention cycle can be applied to immigration to probe how it captured the attention of policymakers. Starting in the late 1970s, it became clear that the 1965 Immigration Act had greatly increased immigration from the Third World. The total number of immigrants allowed in during 1978 was more than double the number in 1965. Yet legal immigration never captured the full attention of the public or the policymakers because, at the same time, illegal immigration increased dramatically (though the vast majority who came to the United States still did so legally). This was the first time in American history that *both* legal and illegal immigration surged simultaneously and were seen as major problems.[15] The media relatively ignored the problems and discontent caused by legal immigration and, instead, devoted most of its attention to illegal immigration. In short, illegal immigration overshadowed legal immigration during the 1970s and beyond.

An examination of *New York Times* articles from 1965 to 1995 reveals how illegal immigration began to dwarf legal immigration on the public agenda during the mid-1970s. Using the *NYT* indexes, the number of immigration articles published each year was counted and divided into four categories: legal immigration, illegal, refugee/asylum, and other.[16]

News events obviously drive media coverage as newspapers report on press conferences, notable incidents, and other newsworthy events. Numerous studies, however, have also suggested that the media themselves through their editorial decisions (e.g., which stories receive front page coverage, the tone of the article, the frequency of articles, the addition of "news analysis" articles, etc.) can affect the public's perceived importance of issues.[17] Many members of the media admit to such bias.[18]

News events fuel coverage, but the media, through its editorial decisions, helps determine what issues are to be perceived as important by the public. The *New York Times*, as the newspaper of record in America, not only helps set the national agenda but it also influences the coverage of local media.[19] Local newspapers, national magazines, and television networks look to the *New York Times* for guidance in assigning their stories and establishing their editorial content. Thus, the *Times*'s coverage can serve as a good indicator of what issues the public will likely perceive to be important and, hence, will reach the policy agenda.

Figure 4.2 shows that the *New York Times* paid very little attention to illegal immigration prior to 1975, while legal immigration received modest coverage. In 1965, only one article was devoted to illegal immigration, but legal immigration received 58 articles. Illegal immigration was not a major problem in 1965, so it is not surprising that the *Times* devoted only one article to it. By 1975—as illegal immigration began to increase—media coverage on illegal immigration increased and had surpassed legal immigration coverage. It would continue to do so for almost every year afterwards. Except for two years in this survey, the number of articles on illegal immigration was higher than that of legal immigration.

Yet why did illegal immigration receive more coverage than legal immigration after 1975 when in reality *both* legal and illegal immigration had increased during the 1970s (and, in fact, the annual number of legal immigrants entering the United States outnumbered illegal immigrants by three to one)? The dynamics of media coverage made the problem of illegal immigration seem worse than it actually was. Illegal immigration is ipso facto illegal, so it is inherently more newsworthy than are stories on legal immigration. Whenever the Border Patrol caught a large group of illegal aliens, it would be immediately covered by the media. A typical article published in January 9, 1980, reported how the Border Patrol captured 500 illegal aliens near San Clemente, California.[20] In the twenty-year survey span, the *NYT* published dozens of this type of account. These brief but constant stories gave a false impression that most people came to the United States illegally because the media understandably did not find it newsworthy to report on the average of 1,500 immigrants who legally entered America every day.[21]

The *New York Times* also published articles whenever INS or Border Patrol officials released statistics on apprehensions. A typical article printed on November 24, 1977, stated that over one million illegal

Figure 4.2
Number of *New York Times* Articles on Legal and Illegal Immigration (1965–1995)

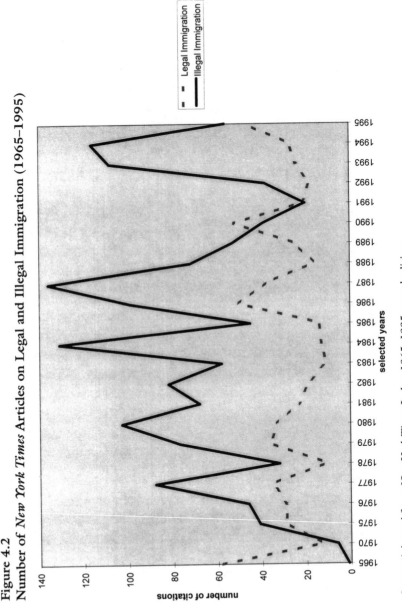

Source: Adapted from *New York Times Index, 1965–1995* annual editions.

aliens had been captured trying to cross the U.S.-Mexico border that year.[22] "The 1,017,000 captured in the year that ended Sept. 30 made up the highest total since 1954," the article ominously noted.[23] A startling figure like one million, without other contextual information (e.g., the number of legal immigrants who have entered, the actual number of illegal aliens who eluded Border Patrol), has the potential to color inaccurately the public's perception about illegal immigration. Then a July 7, 1979, story quoted Border Patrol officials as saying that Mexican aliens were being caught in record numbers.[24] Although the INS kept statistics on the number of apprehensions, it did not have any accurate number of illegal immigrants already residing in the United States. This lack of data led to unreliable estimates. Numbers as high as 12 million illegal aliens were routinely bandied about in news stories. In his December 7, 1978, column, the influential columnist William Safire claimed that over 10 million aliens had entered the United States in recent years.[25] (Later, when more accurate studies were conducted, the actual number of illegal aliens residing in the United States was revised to around 3 to 6 million). All these articles fueled the public perception that there was a crisis in illegal immigration. Consequently, the abundant coverage of illegal immigration (often at the expense of legal immigration) meant that the public became more preoccupied with the illegal problem than with legal immigration.

In addition to the difference in the number of articles, the content of the coverage diverged dramatically for legal and illegal immigration. Illegal immigrants were usually depicted as a burden to society, while articles on legal immigrants were mostly positive. The reasons for this difference can probably be attributed to several factors, including: (1) as a nation that prides itself as being governed by the rule of law, Americans have little sympathy for those who flout immigration laws;[26] (2) illegal immigration is at odds with America's legal immigrant heritage; (3) members of the media—who tend to be more politically liberal and have higher levels of education than the American public— are more likely to view legal immigration sympathetically; and (4) illegal immigrants abusing the system (e.g., welfare) is more newsworthy than legal immigrants doing the same thing because illegal immigrants are, after all, illegal.

Stoking the resentment against illegal immigration were numerous articles that depicted illegal immigrants abusing the social service system. In one article, the *NYT* reported that illegal aliens were receiving federal rent subsidies, "while hundreds of thousands of citizens wait months or years for similar assistance."[27] And one front-page article described how "a tide of illegal immigrants sweeping over the border from Mexico is straining border communities from Texas to California."[28] It went on to quote one local official: "In 18 to 24 months, it's just going to overwhelm the social service system on the border."[29] This is how the media, despite its claim to objectivity, can implicitly persuade the public which issues it should consider important. The front-page treatment and the use of words like "sweeping" and "straining" all work to render a crisis-like illegal immigration situation in the minds of the readers.

The *New York Times* also suggested that illegal aliens may be displacing American workers. A 1975 story pointed out that, "Unlike earlier years, when most illegal aliens worked for substandard wages . . . some of them now earn average and above-average salaries." [30] Such articles countered the common argument that undocumented workers only take jobs that Americans do not want. That interpretation, however, is rather specious: "some" illegal aliens may be earning average or above-average salaries, but another way of phrasing that is to say, "*most* illegal aliens earn below-average salaries." This is yet an additional example of how the media, by parsing one sentence in a particular way, can affect the public's perception. The same theme was echoed five years later in a front-page story.[31] Another 1980 front-page article had a headline that compared illegal aliens to the flow of drugs.[32] Other negative aspects of illegal immigration were stressed as well. A 1975 article, for instance, warned that some "10 to 12 million illegal Mexican aliens . . . increased the danger of Americans contracting tuberculosis."[33]

In contrast, legal immigration received mostly positive coverage. A May 6, 1976, piece detailed how "immigrant Hispanic merchants . . . have revived 11 of 23 stores on 37th Avenue [in Queens], which were vacant a year ago."[34] Other articles examined in the survey celebrated America's immigrant heritage. A 1982 article, for example, reported on plans to restore Ellis Island and create a "living monument" to immigrants.[35] Then, in 1986, a spate of articles commemorated the one hundredth birthday of the Statue of Liberty, with complimentary comments on the contributions of immigrants to America. Only a small handful of articles noted the concerns that many Americans felt about legal immigration. One of the few included a 1986 article that frankly stated that immigration is "altering the political, social and economic fabric of America in a complex way."[36] But that was an exception, not the norm.

Clearly, the rise in illegal immigration during the 1970s was responsible for the heightened media coverage. But the dynamics of media coverage—the manic search for "newsworthy" stories—meant that illegal immigration, because of its illegal nature, received coverage often at the expense of legal immigration. So it is not at all surprising that policymakers decided to pay more attention to illegal immigration rather than legal immigration. Yet Anthony Downs's theory argues that most issues will fade as the public becomes bored or realizes the inordinate costs of solving the problems. Although Downs never stated the duration of the issue-attention cycle, he expected most issues to fade gradually from the public agenda. Illegal immigration, however, has demonstrated remarkable resilience. Except for a couple of off-years, illegal immigration has sustained the public's attention. What explains this longevity? Part of the answer is that illegal immigration continued to increase throughout the 1970s and 1980s. Just as important was that Downs neglected to consider several factors that can substantially increase the length of media coverage: topic differentiation, issue aggregation, and the rise in human interest stories.[37] First, topic differentiation allows the media to give different angles to one topic, producing a flurry of articles over time. In the case of immigration, there were articles on the increase in illegal immigration, on the impact of increased illegal immigration on local communities, on government policy toward increased immigration, and so on. Second, issue aggregation refers to the linkage with other larger concerns. Illegal immigration was linked to welfare, unemployment, cultural change, and a host of other broader issues, giving it a longer life in the media. Finally, "soft" news articles, with a human interest approach supplemented "hard news." So, for example, a "hard" news article on increased illegal immigration could lead to additional, "soft" personal stories on how local communities cope with this problem.

This sustained and abundant media coverage of illegal immigration not only piqued the interest of the general public but also that of policymakers. Legislators began to pay more attention to this issue as constituents complained to their congressmen about illegal immigration. Many of the constituent concerns were probably influenced by the media coverage: constant front-page stories about illegal immigration will galvanize readers. Similarly, interest groups—ranging from labor unions to African-American organizations—lobbied Congress to take action. Not surprisingly, legislators took their cue from their constituents and interest groups and decided to tackle the issue of immigration reform.

THE ILLEGAL AND LEGAL LINK

Restrictionists have found it politically expedient to link illegal and legal immigration together by implying that many of the problems associated with illegal immigration—for example, the use of social services, the displacement of native workers, the degradation of the environment—are similar to those of legal immigration. Senator Alan Simpson, for example, argued on the floor of the Senate that, "If you are talking about reducing immigration, you cannot just talk about illegal immigration. . . . You cannot separate the issue."[38] By blurring the line between legal immigration and the universally detested illegal immigration, restrictionists hope to restructure the debate in their favor. Since the public is overly preoccupied with the relatively new problem of illegal immigration, little attention is paid to legal immigration, and the latter is consequently overshadowed on the public and formal agenda. But if these two issues are linked together, the restrictionists can circumvent the agenda-setting problem. Thus, the original version of the Immigration Reform and Control Act and the 1996 immigration bills contained both anti-illegal immigration and restrictionist legal immigration measures.

Restrictionists had some unexpected help from environmentalists. During the 1970s, consciousness over the environment increased dramatically: Congress passed a slew of environmental protection laws such as the Clean Air Act, and established the Environmental Protection Agency. Also, various private environmental outfits sprouted all across the country. Many of these environmental and population-growth groups questioned the impact of high levels of immigration on the environment. At a Washington, D.C., symposium in 1977, 63 environmental leaders recommended "stabilizing" immigration levels to prevent the degradation of the environment.[39] As Donald Mann, the president of Negative Population Growth put it, "Not only must illegal immigration be halted promptly and completely, but the number of people entering this country legally must be drastically reduced. . . . Immigration, on balance, should not be allowed to further U.S. population growth."[40] And the Environmental Fund produced research claiming that illegal immigration would add 40 million people to the United States population by the year 2000 and require importing

2.3 billion more barrels of oil each year.[41] Most environmental groups did not care if an immigrant came here legally or illegally because both types were seen as a menace to the environment. Their clarion calls to control population growth, however, did not have the overwhelming resonance among the general public because vague, abstract notions like "carry capacity" and "zero population growth" do not click with most people.

The proimmigration bloc in Congress tried to do the exact opposite of what the restrictionists did: they differentiated legal and illegal immigration in stark contrasting terms. Take Senator Edward Kennedy, for example, speaking on the floor of the Senate: "We must not allow our rightful concerns about illegal immigration to create an unwarranted backlash against legal immigrants who enter under our laws, play by the rules, raise their families, pay their taxes and contribute to our communities."[42] In other words, immigration enthusiasts have defended legal immigration by vilifying illegal immigration and harnessing the public anger towards illegal aliens.

Despite the constant efforts of restrictionists, policymakers ultimately focused most of their attention toward illegal immigration when they decided to take up the issue of immigration reform. The constant barrage of media stories on illegal immigration made it their top priority. Furthermore, illegal immigration held the primary position on the agenda because of a sense of crisis. As political scientist James E. Anderson points out, "Items may achieve agenda status and be acted upon as a consequence of crisis or spectacular event."[43] There was a sense that our borders had broken down because of highly publicized cases like the Mariel boat lift debacle in Florida and the constant stories of illegal border crossings in California. Another incentive for tackling illegal immigration only was that legal immigration reform involved a set of more powerful interest groups that opposed any changes. Why bother undertaking the daunting task of legal immigration reform and earn the ire of interest groups when most of the public's attention was focused on illegal immigration?

As early as 1952, a bill penalizing employers who hired illegal aliens had been introduced in Congress, but it foundered because illegal immigration was not perceived of as a major problem then. Bills on illegal immigration started to receive serious consideration only in the early 1970s when Congressman Peter Rodino (D-N.J.) offered bills prohibiting businesses from hiring illegal aliens.[44] His initial bills passed in the House, but they stalled in the Senate subcommittees. Senator

James O. Eastland (D-Mass.), a close ally of agricultural growers, refused to consider the bill. In fact, as the chairman of the Senate Subcommittee on Immigration and Naturalization, Eastland did not even hold a formal meeting on the matter for over ten years![45] Eastland was able to prevent the passage of the bill because of the distribution of power in congressional committees. After legislators revolted against the autocratic style of Speaker of the House Joseph Cannon (dubbed "Cannonism") in 1910, most of the power went to the committee chairmen.[46] The congressional leadership now lacked the power to interfere with the prerogatives of individual committee chairmen, who had free reign over their committees. Until the 1970s, Eastland maintained his fiefdom over immigration policy and refused to consider an illegal immigration bill.

Another complicating factor was that Rodino offered a legalization program along with his employer sanctions proposal. President Jimmy Carter in 1977 followed Rodino's lead and offered his own version of immigration reform, consisting of amnesty and employer sanctions. The amnesty proposal sparked heated debates, and the bill faltered partly because no one knew exactly how many illegal aliens resided in the United States. It was difficult to support amnesty for aliens when no one knew exactly how many people would be legalized. INS commissioner Leonard J. Chapman, for example, testified before a congressional subcommittee that there were anywhere from 4 to 12 million illegal aliens in the United States.[47] Some analysts even assailed the 4 million figure as too high. Hampered by the lack of sufficient data and not eager to address this controversial issue, Congress established the Select Commission on Immigration and Refugee Policy (SCIRP) in 1978 to study the impact of immigration and offer policy proposals. It was a way to both investigate the issue and buy some time.

THE SELECT COMMISSION ON IMMIGRATION AND REFUGEE POLICY

The SCIRP's main purpose was to examine the impact and policy options for illegal immigration, but its charter legislation also included clauses to "review, and make recommendations with respect to the numerical limitations (and exemptions therefrom) of the Immigration and Nationality Act on the admission of permanent resident aliens."[48] The problem of legal immigration played second fiddle to that of illegal immigration.

During its two and a half years of existence, the SCIRP commissioned experts to study the impact of legal and illegal immigration and held numerous hearings across America. On March 1, 1981, the commission issued its recommendations, amid much media attention. The commission enjoyed substantial prestige because of its distinguished bipartisan membership, which included Secretary of Labor F. Ray Marshall, Senator Edward Kennedy, then obscure but well-regarded Senator Alan Simpson, and Representative Peter W. Rodino, Jr., along with several representatives from interest groups. Reverend Theodore M. Hesburgh, the president of the University of Notre Dame, chaired the commission.

The final recommendations of the SCIRP called for immediate action against illegal immigration. Noting that the "Select Commission is well aware of the widespread dissatisfaction among U.S. citizens with an immigrant policy that seems to be out of control," it said the "most pressing" problem of the "half-open door of undocumented/illegal migration should be closed."[49] The commission recommended a three-pronged approach: better border controls; sanctions against employers who hire illegal aliens; and once enforcement mechanisms have been established, legalization of some illegal aliens already in the United States.

The report also explicitly linked legal and illegal immigration, but not in the way hoped for by restrictionists. The commission recommended "closing the back door to undocumented/illegal migration" to allow "opening the front door a little more to accommodate legal migration in the interests of the country."[50] In other words, it was a variation of the proimmigration theme: illegal immigration, bad; legal immigration, good. This recommendation was not surprising, considering that the vast majority of the sixteen members of the commission held pro-immigration views.[51] Four of the members were Democratic congressmen generally sympathetic to legal immigration; the next four were chosen by President Carter, who was also generally proimmigration; another four were members of Carter's cabinet; and the remaining four were Republican congressmen, most of whom were of the pro-growth, libertarian view. Only Senator Alan Simpson could be considered to have restrictionist views.

Despite its proimmigration tilt, the commission urged caution in legal immigration reform. Noting that we cannot "become a land of unlimited immigration," the report stressed that, "This is not the time for large-scale expansion in legal immigration. . . . The Commission is, therefore, recommending a modest increase in legal immigration sufficient to expedite the clearance of backlogs—mainly to reunify families—which have developed under the current immigration system and to introduce a new system, which we believe will be more equitable and more clearly reflect our interests as a nation."[52] Policy-wise, it meant advocating an increase in the annual numerically limited ceiling from 270,000 to 350,000 and an addition of 100,000 more visas for the next five years to clear the backlogs. It also called for a two-tier system of immigration for family-based visas and "independent" (i.e., nonfamily-based) visas. But this recommendation needs to be seen in conjunction with the illegal immigration proposal. It was not an invitation to greatly open the country's border, as some have suggested. Rather, the commission was pushing for a modest increase in legal immigration only on the condition that illegal immigration be substantially decreased. Thus, the commission was hoping that net immigration to the United States would remain the same if its policies were implemented.

The SCIRP's recommendations served as the blueprint for future legislation: the 1986 Immigration Reform and Control Act to deal with illegal immigration, and the 1990 Immigration Act to reform legal immigration.

THE FATE OF IRCA

The Immigration Reform and Control Act of 1986 had a torturous and tumultuous path to its passage.[53] After the SCIRP's final report was announced in March 1981, the Reagan administration established a special presidential task force to examine the commission's findings and finally drafted a bill later in 1981, which roughly conformed to the SCIRP's recommendations. That bill never received much attention because Senator Alan Simpson (R-Wyo.) and Representative Romano Mazzoli (D-NJ), the chairmen of the Senate and House Judiciary subcommittees on immigration and both members of the SCIRP, offered their own versions of the bill. Both versions contained the basic framework outlined in the SCIRP's final report: they suggested imposing sanctions against employers who hire illegal aliens and offered a legalization program. Alan Simpson placed a firmer cap on legal immigration in the Senate bill. The proposed cap was set at 425,000: 350,000 for family members and 75,000 for special, nonfamily immigrants. The number of immediate family members (who were normally exempt from any caps) would have been subtracted from the 350,000 family-reunification visas, placing a firmer cap on immigration. The proposed 425,000 ceiling would have reduced immigration; in 1980, nearly 600,000 immigrants had entered. Such a cap also existed in the House bill, but it was removed during the House committee mark-ups. The Senate was controlled by the Republicans in 1982, so Simpson had an easier time swaying his colleagues not to tamper with his bill. The House, on the other hand, was controlled by Democrats, who were solicitous to ethnic groups that opposed legal immigration caps. Consequently, the caps were quickly removed.

The Senate passed Simpson's bill, but the House version foundered on the floor of Congress as legislators placed hundreds of amendments. Hispanic groups, business lobbyists, and agricultural businesses all found fault in provisions like employer sanctions. Time ran out in the 97th Congress before legislators could sort through all the amendments. The 98th Congress took up the bill again, but the bill never materialized out of the conference agreement because the conferees could not come to agreement over antidiscrimination and funding issues. The conference, though, agreed to scuttle the Senate's yearly cap because the conferees believed that the bill, which was already rife with contention, should not be complicated further by legal immigration reform. The third time was a charm as the Immigration Reform and Control Act finally passed in the waning days of the 99th Congress. Flustered by the previous two failed attempts, neither the House nor the Senate bills bothered to include any provisions on legal immigration. That would have to wait until 1990.

The fate of the legal immigration provisions in the IRCA should give a flavor of immigration politics: illegal immigration often obscures legal immigration, and politicians find it expedient to ignore legal immigration reform. A more in-depth examination of the link between legal and illegal immigration will be discussed in a future chapter, but it should be clearly noted that the increase in illegal immigration had altered the context and structure of the debate over legal immigration reform. Had illegal immigration not increased during the 1970s, it is quite possible that policymakers would have had to answer to the public discontent and curtailed legal immigration. But the imposition of ceilings in 1965 and 1976 had the unforeseen consequence of increasing illegal immigration, which had the unintended effect of changing the framework of immigration politics. Such is the irony of public policy.

NOTES

1. United States Congress, Senate Committee on the Judiciary, *U.S. Immigration Law and Policy: 1952–1979*, 96th Congress, 1st Session (1979), pp. 234–42.

2. David M. Reimers, *Still the Golden Door: The Third World Comes to America* (New York: Columbia University Press, 1992), p. 85.

3. Ibid., p. 86.

4. United States Congress, Senate Committee on the Judiciary, *U.S. Immigration Law and Policy: 1952–1986*, 100th Congress, 1st Session (1987), p. 39.

5. Reimers, *Golden Door*, p. 44.

6 Senate Committee, *U.S. Immigration 1952–1986*, p. 42.

7. United States Immigration and Naturalization Service, *Statistical Yearbook of the Immigration and Naturalization Service, 1994* (Washington, D.C.: U.S. Government Printing Office, 1996), p. 179.

8. Note that these figures might inflate the number of illegal immigrants who entered the United States because many of them undoubtedly were apprehended on numerous occasions. Furthermore, most of the apprehensions occur at the border—internal apprehensions are far too difficult and sparse—so the figure probably inflates the number of Mexican apprehensions.

9. INS, *Yearbook*, p. 160.

10. Reimers, *Open Door*, p. 53.

11. Ibid., p. 53.

12. David M. Reimers, "Recent Immigration Policy: An Analysis," Barry R. Chiswick, ed., *The Gateway: U.S. Immigration Issues and Policies* (Washington, D.C.: American Enterprise Institute, 1982), p. 47.

13. Roger Cobb, Jennie-Keith Ross, and Marc Howard Ross, "Agenda Building as a Comparative Political Process," *The American Political Science Review* 70 (1976): p. 126.

14. Anthony Downs, "Up and Down with Ecology: The 'Issue-Attention Cycle,' " David L. Protess and Maxwell McCombs, eds., *Agenda Setting: Readings on Media, Public Opinion and Policymaking* (Hillsdale, N.J.: Erlbaum, 1991), p. 27. Downs used the environmental movement as an example of how public intensity has declined over the years. Downs, however, qualified his issue-attention cycle, arguing that not all social problems undergo this cycle. See the article for a more elaborate discussion.

15. Illegal immigration had received serious policy consideration in the 1950s when legal immigration was relatively low, but it soon faded out of the public agenda after the success of Operation Wetback.

16. Any story that dealt with legal immigration policy or legal immigrants was considered a "legal immigration" story. The same process was repeated for illegal immigration. The categorization of the articles is admittedly somewhat subjective. Some stories can fit into both categories; others do not fit

either. The point of this exercise was not precisely to tally the number of articles in each area, but rather to show the broader, general trend in media coverage. Letters to the editor were not considered articles.

17. For example, see Wayne Wanta and Yu-Wei Hu, "Time-Lag Differences in the Agenda-Setting Process: An Examination of Five News Media," *International Journal of Public Opinion* 6 (1994): 225–40.

18. For example, William Powers, the former media writer at *The New Republic* and *Washington Post*, has argued that the national media, despite devoting news stories on the Clinton scandals, has sent an implicit message that these stories are not truly important or newsworthy. See William Powers, "Scandal-shy," *The New Republic*, 16 December 1996, pp. 24–26.

19. Wanta and Hu, "Time-Lag Differences," 225–40.

20. "Augmented Border Patrol Seizes 500 Illegal Aliens," *New York Times*, 9 January 1980, p. 14.

21. Most polls show that most Americans think illegal immigration is the main source of immigration.

22. "More than Million Aliens Caught at Mexican Border," *New York Times*, 24 November 1977, p. A16.

23. Ibid., p. A16.

24. "Illegal Aliens from Mexico Being Seized at Record Pace," *New York Times*, 7 July 1979, p. 6.

25. William Safire, "The News of '79," *New York Times*, 7 December 1978, p. A23.

26. For example, see Lawrence H. Fuchs, "The Search for a Sound Immigration Policy: A Personal View," Nathan Glazer, ed., *Clamor at the Gates* (San Francisco: ICS Press, 1985), p. 21.

27. Robert Pear, "Congressional Inquiry Finds Aliens Getting Federal Subsidies for Rents," *New York Times*, 16 March, 1981, p. A13.

28. Peter Applebome, "Surge of Illegal Aliens Taxes Southwest Towns' Resources," *New York Times*, 9 March 1986, p. 1.

29. Ibid., p. 1.

30. Peter B. Flint, "Rise Seen in Pay to Illegal Aliens in State," *New York Times*, 22 February 1975, p. 58.

31. John M. Crewdson, "Illegal Aliens are Bypassing Farms for Higher Pay of Jobs in the Cities," *New York Times*, 10 November, 1980, p. A1.

32. John M. Crewdson, "Smugglers Find Aliens as Valuable as Drugs Along Mexican Border," *New York Times*, 15 July 1980, p. A1.

33. "TB Rise Sparked by Illegal Aliens," *New York Times*, 18 May 1975, p. 34.

34. Murray Schumach, "Enterprising Hispanic Merchants Revive a Block in Jackson Heights," *New York Times*, 6 May 1976, p. 39.

35. Richard Bernstein, "For Ellis Island, A Reborn Role as a Monument," *New York Times*, 9 December 1982, p. B1.

36. Robert Reinhold, "Flow of 3rd World Immigrants Alters Weave of U.S. Society," *New York Times,* 30 June 1986, p. A1.

37. Barbara Nelson, "Making an Issue of Child Abuse," David L. Protess and Maxwell McCombs, eds., *Agenda Setting: Readings on Media, Public Opinion and Policymaking* (Hillsdale, N.J.: Erlbaum, 1991), p. 165.

38. *Congressional Record,* 25 April 1996, p. S4120.

39. "63 Environmentalists Urge 'Gas' Tax Rise, with Curb on Population and Smoking," *New York Times,* February 3, 1977, p. 19.

40. Donald Mann, "Immigration Should Not Be Allowed to Further U.S. Population Growth," letter to the editor, *New York Times,* 26 August 1977, p. 28.

41. James W. Singer, "The Virtues of Procrastination," *National Journal,* 12 May 1979, p. 795.

42. *Congressional Record,* April 15, 1996, p. S3283.

43. James E. Anderson, *Public Policy-Making* (New York: Praeger, 1975), p. 61.

44. Michael D. Hoefer, "Background on U.S. Immigration Policy Reform," Francisco L. Rivera-Batiz, Selig L. Sechzer, and Ira N. Gang, eds., *U.S. Immigration Policy Reform in the 1980s: A Preliminary Assessment* (New York: Praeger, 1991), p. 18. The Walter-McCarran Act made it illegal to "harbor" illegal aliens, but the "Texas Proviso"—an infamous clause attached by pro-grower legislators—exempted hiring illegal aliens from the definition of "harboring."

45. Richard D. Lyons, "Seldom Active Senate Unit Drew $2–Million in Decade," *New York Times,* 29 September 1975, p. 1.

46. Roger H. Davidson and Walter J. Oleszek, *Congress and Its Members* (Washington, D.C.: Congressional Quarterly Press, 1994), p. 207.

47. Barry Edmonston, Jeffrey S. Passel, and Frank D. Bean, "Perceptions and Estimates of Undocumented Migration to the United States," Bean, Edmonston, and Passel, eds., *Undocumented Migration to the United States: IRCA and the Experience of the 1980s* (Washington, D.C.: Urban Institute, 1990), p. 16.

48. SCIRP, *Final Report,* p. xi.

49. Ibid., p. 10, 35.

50. Ibid., p. 3.

51. The sixteen members of the commission were: Reverend Theodore Hesburgh, the president of Notre Dame; Rose Ochi of the mayor's office in Los Angeles; Joaquin Otero, vice president of the Brotherhood of Railway and Airline Clerks; Jose Cruz Reynoso, associate justice of the California Court of Appeals; Attorney General Benjamin Civiletti; Secretary of Health and Human Services Patricia Roberts Harris; Secretary of Labor F. Ray Marshall; Secretary of State Edmund S. Muskie; Senators Dennis DeConcini, Edward Kennedy, Charles Mathias, and Alan K. Simpson; and Repre-

sentatives Hamilton Fish, Elizabeth Holtzman, Robert McClory, and Peter Rodino, Jr.

52. SCIRP, *Final Report*, pp. 9–10.

53. The synopsis of the bills' path to passage is based mainly on various *Congressional Quarterly Weekly Reports* and *New York Times* articles.

Chapter 5

The Elite and the State: Common Explanations for the Immigration Puzzle

"I don't want to sound like a Marxist, but the largest economic result of high immigration is that it brings a lot of poor workers here, so the rich can benefit from it, while the poor and the middle-class do not," says Skip Garling, the director of research and publications at Federation of American Immigration Reform (FAIR), the leading restrictionist organization.[1] Garling, like many other restrictionists, complains that big business has tremendous power in shaping immigration policy at the expense of the general public. This idea of hegemonic big businesses bringing in millions of immigrants for cheap labor is a commonly held belief among many Americans. Indeed, popular culture is rife with stories of big business engaging in rapacious, conspiratorial schemes. Many scholars lend credence to this commonly held view. Class-based elite theorists claim that a small cadre of advanced capitalists hold the most powerful positions in society and have tremendous influence over public policy, often against the wishes of the masses. As political scientist C. Wright Mills explains, "The power elite is composed of men whose positions enable them to transcend the ordinary environments of ordinary men and women; they are in positions to make decisions having major consequences."[2]

It is not surprising that businesses would putatively want high levels of immigration: a larger labor pool depresses wages and weakens the leverage power of organized workers vis-à-vis the capital holders. A cursory examination of the three immigration laws—the 1986 Immigration Reform and Control Act, the Immigration Act of 1990, and the 1996 immigration legislation—seems to corroborate the elite theory. The Senate version of the IRCA (S. 2222 and S. 529) placed a more firm numerical ceiling on legal immigration, but that provision was eventually stripped, proving to elite theorists that business got its way. In the final version of the bill, Congress, at the prodding of large agri-businesses, added a highly controversial amnesty program for illegal aliens. Congressman William Dannemeyer (R-Calif.) explained, "If we do not give amnesty . . . the day after we have sanctions we are not going to have anybody working."[3]

The Immigration Act of 1990, in particular, seems to prove that big business dominates policy-making at the expense of the mass public. Not only did the legislation increase annual immigration levels by nearly 40%, it nearly tripled employer-based quotas from 55,000 to 140,000 and created a special investor program to grant visas to entrepreneurs willing to invest one million dollars in the United States. Legislators were frank in their solicitude toward businesses during debate on the floor of Congress. "American companies have difficulty recruiting high skilled workers who have crucial knowledge of international markets and pioneer research. . . . How do we expect America to remain competitive if our companies, who often face labor shortages in this country, can't recruit the best talent and top notch researchers from abroad," complained Jesse Helms, who is not generally known for his proimmigration views.[4] He later explained, "I cannot tell you how many calls and letters I have had from my own State from business and industry saying we need help bringing in more skilled workers."[5] Added Congressman Bill Richardson (D-N.M.): "The reason this bill is important is because it is good for American business, it is good for American global competition."[6]

The failure of Congressman Lamar Smith's and Senator Alan Simpson's restrictive immigration bills in 1996—despite popular public support for them—appears to further strengthen the thesis that big business is responsible for high levels of immigration. Both bills did not have support from the business community, which helped railroad their passage. On the floor of the Senate, Alan Simpson caustically blamed Grover Norquist, the head of the libertarian Americans for Tax Reform, and big business for conspiring to kill his bill: "Uncle Grover . . . is getting paid 10,000 bucks a month by Mr. [Bill] Gates of Microsoft to mess up the issue. And he has done a magnificent job of messing up the issue and should for 10,000 bucks a month."[7]

The key problem with elite theory, however, is that it grossly inflates the power of business. Although business undoubtedly wields substantial influence, it is not hegemonic. Nonbusiness interest groups can play important roles as well. In fact, from 1921 to 1965, business constantly lost its policy battles to non-business interest groups as Congress enacted very restrictionist measures. And businesses have not gotten their way in other areas such as environmental regulation. Elite theory cannot convincingly explain why this happened. Some structuralist elite theorists argue that the working class may occasionally "win" to maintain the legitimacy of the system and stave off demands for serious, radical changes in society. But this argument is circular and really is no argument at all: no matter what the outcome, it automatically assumes that big business is responsible.

Furthermore, "big business" is not monolithic. Businesses, depending on their size and industry, hold diverging views on immigration. Highly capital-based industries are rather indifferent toward immigration policy, whereas labor-based industries play an active role because they are more dependent on foreign labor. Even among immigration supporters, businesses advocate different types of immigration, depending on their industry and needs. The Chamber of Commerce, which represents primarily small businesses, supported the creation of a program that granted visas to foreign investors willing to invest $1 million in the United States. On the other hand, the National Association of Manufacturers, whose membership consists primarily of big businesses, was neutral on this aspect. The reason for this difference is rooted in their different interests: the Chamber of Commerce's political clout can increase if an investor visa program attracts capital to create small businesses in the United States, whereas large corporations gain little from having a foreigner invest a "measly" one million dollars in a small business.

Elite theory, despite its propensity to exaggerate the power of business, still has merit: it perspicaciously focuses on the impressive but limited influence of business in public policy. Pluralist theorists often ignore this aspect. So what we need is a modified pluralist framework that admits that businesses are very influential in a market-based society but also concedes that nonbusiness interest groups can often successfully counteract big business.

Even if we accepted the central tenet of elite theory that big business has preponderant power in policy-making, it fails to explain fully the high levels of immigration because it cannot explain family-based immigration. Business concentrates most of its lobbying efforts on skills-based immigration policy—which accounts for a mere 20% of all visas—and ignores family-based immigration. Another theory is required to explain how the other 80% of the visas are maintained. During congressional hearings for the Immigration Act of 1990, virtually all the business representatives spoke in favor of increased employment-related immigration and streamlined labor certification procedures, but very few groups mentioned family-based immigration. For example, Daryl Buffenstein of the Chamber of Commerce complained to Congress that, "only 20 percent of the present immigration quota . . . is related to employment, while 80 percent is devoted to family immigration. . . . There is a need for balanced reform, which recognizes the needs of business and industry by increasing, in absolute terms, the quota applicable to business-related immigration."[8] The National Association of Manufacturers paid little attention to family-based immigration and instead lobbied for an "expeditious set of immigration policies for the transfer of international personnel as well as the ability to bring in the necessary number of foreign experts for training and project development."[9] Other business groups, like the Business and Employers Coalition and the American Council on International Personnel, echoed the same theme.

An analysis of voting patterns of Republicans and Democrats shows the limits of elite theory. Republicans should be as proimmigration as Democrats (if not more so) because the GOP clearly represents the more probusiness party, whether measured in ideological terms or in campaign donations received from business groups. Indeed, the Democratic Party should oppose immigration because it is more solicitous to the interests of labor. Yet it was a Republican Congress that proposed curbing immigration in 1996 and a Democratic Congress that expanded immigration in 1990. That hints toward a more pluralist explanation: there are other pressures and factors (such as constituent wishes and lobbying from nonbusiness groups) that help explain the behavior of legislators. Some Republicans, despite their laissez-faire leanings, might vote to restrict immigration because of cultural concerns that immigration might be ethnically balkanizing the country. And Democrats may vote to increase immigration because of pressure from ethnic groups, a large constituency of the Democratic coalition.

How members of Congress voted by party on specific amendments during Judiciary Committee mark-ups for three bills—the 1996 immigration bills (H.R. 2202 and S. 1664) and the Immigration and Reform Control bill of 1982 (S. 2222)—was examined. These three committee mark-ups were chosen because they were the only ones with specific votes for each amendment in their committee reports. The virtue of examining specific amendments is that it is easier to distill a member's views on immigration because, unlike a full bill, it is not cluttered with other provisions or amendments. In addition to these committee amendments, the floor amendments for the IRCA, the Immigration Act of 1990, and the 1996 immigration legislation were examined.

Time and time again, it was the putatively probusiness (and hence proimmigration) Republicans, who wanted to restrict family-based visas, while the less probusiness Democrats voted to maintain high levels of immigration (see table 5.1). It should, however, be noted that there are many fiscally conservative Republicans, like Senator Spencer Abraham, who are ardent immigration supporters, and, likewise, there are Democrats (usually Southern) who vote along restrictionist lines. But, on the whole, party voting has been contrary to elite theory expectations. For example, in the 1982 Judiciary Committee, Senator Edward Kennedy offered an amendment to restore the fifth preference category for adult brothers and sisters of U.S. citizens into the original Senate bill. Seven Republicans and one Democrat voted against the amendment, while four Democrats and no Republican voted in favor of it. Likewise, on the floor in 1996, nearly two-thirds of the House Republicans voted to keep the restrictionist legal immigration provision in the bill, while the vast majority of Democrats voted to kill that section.

Thus, lobbying by business groups may explain why Congress expanded employment-based immigration from 55,000 to 140,000 a year in 1990, but it fails to elucidate why family-based immigration increased and why the "diversity" program was established. Apparently, other pressures and forces other than business were at work. Ironically, although the 1990 act was heralded by the media and Congress as a pro-business legislation, the increase in family-based and "diversity" visas meant that employment-based visas as a percentage of total immigration remained the same (at 20%) as originally set by the 1965 Immigration Act. So we see the limits of elite theory as a comprehensive explanation for high levels of immigration: business is primarily involved in only one-fifth of the visas, and, thus, elite theory can at most only be a partial explanation.

The 1996 immigration bill is a particularly good case study of the role of business in immigration policy. Because the restrictionist thrust of the bill posed a threat to business interests, it is instructive to examine how business reacted. During the committee mark-ups and floor voting, business groups exerted intense pressure on Congress to remove the proposed reductions in employment-based immigration but were silent on cuts in family-based immigration. Austin T. Fragomen, Jr., the chairman of the American Council on International Personnel, devoted scant attention to the proposed extensive reductions in family-based immigration. "We have consistently maintained that employment-based immigration should be kept separate from family-sponsored immigration," said Fragomen, in his plea to save employment-based immigration

Table 5.1
Judiciary Committee Amendment Voting and Floor Amendment Voting

Amendment	GOP (yes)	GOP (no)	Dem. (yes)	Dem. (no)
COMMITTEE VOTING				
H.R. 2202 (1996)				
Berman Amend: strike restrictive legal provisions	1	18	13	2
Lee Amend: eliminate cap and restore family visas	2	15	14	1
Schumer Amend: restore diversity programs	5	11	13	0
Becerra Amend: Decrease income req't for sponsors	0	13	6	1
S. 1664 (1996)				
Abraham Amend: separate legal and illegal provisions	6	4	6	2
S. 2222 (1982)				
Kennedy Amend: restore 5th Preference visas	0	7	4	1
Kennedy Amend: delete req't lowering family visas	0	7	5	0
Metzenbaum Amend: Expand 3rd Preference	0	8	5	0
FLOOR VOTING				
H.R. 2202 (1996)				
Chrysler-Brownback Amend: Delete restrictive legal immigration provisions. Passed 238-183	75	158	162	25
H.R. 4300 (1990)				
Smith Amend: Recommit expansive bill to committee, killing it. Rejected 176-248	137	35	39	213
Smith Amend: Set firmer 630,000 ceiling. Rejected 143-266.	104	56	39	210
H.R. 1510 (1984)				
Moorhead Amend: Set firmer 450,000 annual cap on immigration. Rejected 168-231	111	46	57	185

Source: Congressional Quarterly Almanac (1984, 1989, 1990 annual editions), various issues of *Congressional Quarterly Weekly Report*, and various reports by the U.S. Senate Committee on the Judiciary.

from the Republican restrictionists in Congress.[10] David Pritchard, the director of recruiting at Microsoft, admitted that the multibillion dollar computer software corporation is mostly concerned with skills-based immigration, in particular the H-1B temporary worker programs.[11] Kirby Dyess, the vice president of Human Resources at Intel, is also not overly concerned with mass immigration. "Only about one percent of our workers are immigrants specifically brought to work [here]," she said.[12]

Despite the pleas by business, the Senate bill was especially draconian on business-related visas: it reduced skills-based visas from 140,000 to 90,000 and set a $10,000-per-head tax on immigrant workers brought by businesses. This elicited a quick and harsh response. Business groups, led by the powerful National Association of Manufacturers, held a special press conference to excoriate Senator Simpson's immigration bill.[13] "This country is not producing the workers we need to be globally competitive," said Jeff Joseph, a vice president at the U.S. Chamber of Commerce.[14] Amidst all this political pressure, Simpson, whose real target was the visa-rich family-reunification policy, decided it would be politically expedient to try to buy off business opposition and offered to drop all restrictions on both permanent and temporary employment programs.

The House bill was more modest than the Senate version. In addition to reducing slightly employment-based visas from 140,000 to 135,000, it placed stricter restrictions on the use of the H-1B temporary worker program. Business groups, nevertheless, opposed the bill. After being intensely lobbied, immigration subcommittee chairman and author of the bill, Representative Lamar Smith, reluctantly removed most of the restrictions.[15] Once these employment-based restrictions were deleted, the National Association of Manufacturers promised not to lobby to remove or separate the legal immigration reform provisions from the illegal immigration part.[16] In other words, the National Association of Manufacturers would not unduly interfere with the House bill's plan to cut family-based immigration as long as the House did not touch employment-based immigration. As far as business was concerned, Congress could cut immigration by 80% and it would not care as long the business-related visas were retained. In fact, in some cases, some businesses actually supported reductions in family-based immigration. For example, Intel and Hewlett-Packard initially lobbied against the Brownback-Chrysler amendment, which would have removed cuts in the family-based immigration provisions from the bill.[17]

Some observers may argue that the defeat of the restrictionist bills in 1996 and the concessions given to businesses confirm the elite theory that businesses have tremendous influence over public policy. Admittedly, businesses are very powerful, but it should be noted that very few interest groups opposed businesses in the 1990 or 1996 immigration battles. Nonbusiness groups found it politically expedient to form a coalition and work with businesses. Had powerful nonbusiness groups actively opposed skills-based visas, business groups might not have triumphed. Thus, the victory for business might be attributable to coalition politics, not necessarily to the hegemony of business. The difference between a pluralist framework and an elite one can sometimes be blurry. The main difference lies in their emphases: elite theory focuses on class, while a pluralist view encompasses broader factors. A modified pluralist theory that takes into account both the power and limits of capital can provide a more accurate and nuanced description of how immigration policy is established.

A FOREIGN POLICY PREROGATIVE?

Another common explanation for the high levels of immigration is the foreign policy prerogative: the United States must pay attention to foreign policy considerations, compelling the government to maintain a generous immigration policy. Among scholars, the state-as-actor/realist theory, which helps explain this foreign policy prerogative, has gained increased prominence in recent years. In contrast to the pluralist notion of the state as a neutral arbiter of different private interest groups, the state-as-actor theory—popularized by political scientists like Theda Skocpol—argues that the state is an autonomous actor with its own independent interests and, accordingly, plays an active role in the policy-making arena. The state theory would point to the president's foreign policy imperatives to explain immigration policy. As a superpower nation and an important player in global politics, the United States cannot afford to alienate other countries by enacting discriminatory or draconian immigration policy. A generous immigration policy represents a gesture of goodwill toward other nations.

The state theory is most cogent in explaining the institutional differences between the president and the Congress on immigration. It is almost always Congress, which represents local, parochial interests, that pushes for restrictions, while the president, who must pay attention to national foreign policy concerns, prefers a more liberal immigration policy. State considerations have historically played an important role in the development of immigration policy. From Chester Arthur's opposition to the Chinese Exclusionary Act to Woodrow Wilson's rejection of literacy tests to Harry Truman's veto of the Walter-McCarran Act, the president has almost always resisted Congress's attempts to close the doors to foreigners.

The state theory is equally powerful in explaining the establishment of refugee policy. Before World War II, the United States did not have a separate legal category called "refugees." It was only after World War II—when the United States assumed an active role in geopolitics—that a special refugee status was established, at the prodding of the State Department. Once this legal category was set, the president took a leading role in this refugee policy during the Cold War. Despite occasional protests from Congress, the president has repeatedly used the parole authority power to accept refugees, most of whom were fleeing communist regimes. For example, the president allowed in hundreds of thousands of refugees from Vietnam after the fall of Saigon. In recent years, the United States has accepted a large influx of refugees from Eastern Europe.

As intimated by state theory, America's global leadership almost definitely precludes the enactment of deep reductions in immigration or refugee quotas. Yet, it is less convincing in other ways. Why did the United States increase immigration levels in the 1990 act? Did increasing immigration by 40% increase the efficacy of foreign policy by 40%? Surely not. Indeed, the "state"—as represented by the State, Labor and Justice departments—was averse to large increases in immigration. President George Bush expressed concern over the House's generous immigration bill, which would have raised the annual levels to over 800,000. Gene McNary, the Immigration and Naturalization commissioner, told Congress, "While the Administration supports a moderate increase in the level of second preference immigration, we believe that these bills go far beyond a moderate increase."[18] He also testified that the administration only wanted an increase in skills-based immigration and preferred family preference immigration to remain the same.

Other administration officials were vociferously opposed to the House bill. "We cannot support proposals that would exempt spouses and minor children of U.S. permanent residents from numerical limitations, and thereby dramatically increase overall levels of immigration. The Administration's opposition to such proposals stems from concerns about the potentially disruptive effect of these much larger numbers of immigrants on both ongoing labor market adjustments and wages and job opportunities of U.S. workers," warned David O. Williams, a deputy assistant secretary of labor.[19] Erich Pratt, the executive director of the U.S. Border Control, also testified against the bill because of its generous increase.[20] Bush himself warned Congress that he would veto a bill modeled after the House version.

In fact, a generous immigration policy can sometimes conflict with the foreign policy goals of the United States if it encourages "brain drain" from other countries. Representative John Bryant (D-Tex.) worried that there might be a "brain drain or a capital drain from areas of the world which we are going to turn right back around and support through our foreign policies, foreign aid, and trade policies."[21] Princeton N. Lyman, the director of the Bureau for Refugee Programs of the State Department, agreed: "I think in fashioning immigration legislation, one wants to keep in mind a balance between a magnet for brain drain on the one hand, and on the other hand meeting U.S. interests and needs in a world in which many people are going to be moving and in a world in which there is a good deal of migration."[22]

These testimonies weaken the state-as-actor notion that the state is responsible for high levels of immigration. It probably explains why immigration will not fall below a certain level, but it fails to explain convincingly why immigration cannot be reduced moderately (say, by one-third).

Indeed, when Congress proposed curtailing immigration by a third in 1996, administration officials did not actively oppose the proposals. During the congressional hearings, representatives from the INS, the State Department, the Labor Department, and the Justice Department said little in regards to the legal immigration proposals. Most of the criticisms were directed toward other provisions in the bill, such as changes in refugee policy and illegal alien employer verification proposals. Moreover, both President Bill Clinton and Republican presidential candidate Robert Dole approved the United States Commission on Immigration Reform's recommendation to curtail immigration by a third.

CONCLUSIONS

Foreign policy and business clout both help explain why immigration levels are high, but they only answer a part of the puzzle. Elite theory incisively stresses the power that businesses have in policy-making.

Pluralists sometimes fail to emphasize this enough. But elite theory tends to overstate the influence of businesses and ignores the power of nonbusiness interest groups. The state-as-actor theory similarly does an effective job in elucidating the role of foreign policy in immigration policy. But it is not as persuasive in explaining why there cannot be moderate decreases in immigrants. The rest of the immigration puzzle is best explained by a modified pluralist framework of coalition politics.

NOTES

1. Interviewed by author, April 11, 1997.
2. C. Wright Mill, *The Power Elite* (New York: Oxford University Press, 1959), pp. 3–4.
3. "Bill to Curb Illegal Immigration: House Debate Reflects Diversity of Nation," *New York Times*, 17 June 1984, p. 21.
4. *Congressional Record*, 12 July 1989, p. S14268.
5. *Congressional Record*, 13 July 1990, p. S14531.
6. *Congressional Record*, 2 October 1990, p. H8645.
7. *Congressional Record*, 25 April 1996, p. S4120.
8. United States Congress, The House Subcommittee on Immigration, Refugees, and International Law of the Committee on the Judiciary, *Immigration Act of 1989 (Part 1): Hearings*, 101st Congress, 1st Session, 1989, pp. 444–45.
9. Ibid., p. 476.
10. United States Congress, The House Subcommittee on Immigration and Claims of the Committee on the Judiciary, *Immigration in the National Interest Act of 1995: Hearings*, 104th Congress, 1st Session, 1995, p. 99.
11. Interviewed by author, August 1996.
12. Interviewed by author, August 1996.
13. Holly Idelson, "Business Lobbies Fighting Foreign Worker Curbs," *Congressional Quarterly Weekly Report*, 25 November 1995, pp. 3600–601.
14. Ibid., p. 3601.
15. Holly Idelson, "House Judiciary Approves Sweeping Restrictions," *Congressional Quarterly Weekly Report*, 28 October 1995, p. 3305.
16. Holly Idelson, "Economic Anxieties Bring Debate on Immigration to a Boil," *Congressional Quarterly Weekly Report*, 16 March 1996, p. 701.
17. Interviewed by author, March 31, 1997.
18. United States Congress, The House Subcommittee on Immigration, Refugees and International Law of the Committee on the Judiciary, *Immigration Act of 1989 (Part 2):Hearings*, 101st Congress, 2d Session, 1990, p. 38.
19. United States Congress, The House Subcommittee on Immigration, Refugees and International Law of the Committee on the Judiciary, and Immi-

gration Task Force of the Committee on Education and Labor, *Immigration Act of 1989 (Part 3): Hearings,* 101st Congress, 2d Session, 1990, p. 6.

20. Ibid., p. 842.
21. House Subcommittee, *Immigration Act of 1989 (Part 2),* p. 60.
22. Ibid., p. 60–61.

Chapter 6

The Left-Right Alliance

When Congressman Lamar Smith (R-Tex.) introduced his "Immigration in the National Interest Act of 1995" in the summer of that year, a comprehensive immigration reform seemed imminent and inevitable. Public discontent over the post-1965 immigration policy had hit its apogee: opinion polls revealed that nearly two-thirds of Americans wanted to reduce immigration levels. The public's anger over the "immigration invasion" was palpable in 1994 when nearly two-thirds of California voters passed Proposition 187, a measure that would cut off all public assistance for illegal immigrants. Representative Smith's bill, the first thoroughly restrictionist proposal to receive serious consideration in nearly seventy years, would have curtailed legal immigration by one-third and taken harsher measures against illegal immigration. "To wait any longer would put us on the wrong side of the American people, on the wrong side of common sense, and on the wrong side of our responsibility as legislators," declared Smith, the chairman of the House Judiciary Subcommittee on Immigration and Claims.[1] John Bryant (D-Tex.), the ranking minority member of the immigration subcommittee, concurred: "This is a problem that we can no longer ignore."[2] A couple of months after the introduction of Smith's bill, Senator Alan Simpson (R-Wyo.), the chair of the Senate's immigration subcommittee, promulgated his own immigration proposal, which was even more draconian than Smith's bill. Gone from the

chairs of the immigration subcommittees were proimmigration legislators like Senator Edward Kennedy and Representative Bruce Morrison;
now, they were headed by bonafide restrictionists, Lamar Smith and
Alan Simpson.

The political climate surely appeared propitious for serious immigration reform. Both the general public and the political elites seemed to
agree that legal immigration needed to be reduced. A large impetus for
immigration reform came from the Commission on Immigration
Reform, a nine-member committee appointed by the president and the
Congress, as mandated by the 1990 Immigration Act. The commission,
chaired by former Democratic Congresswoman Barbara Jordan, was
inaugurated to examine the effects of the 1990 Immigration Act and
offer policy proposals for both legal and illegal immigration. After
spending several years examining the current immigration policy, the
committee, much like Smith's and Simpson's bills, recommended
reducing immigration by about a third and taking a tougher stand
against illegal immigration. This final report carried considerable
weight among policymakers because of the commission's distinguished
bipartisan membership. Furthermore, the report could not be easily
impugned as nativist screed because of Jordan's impeccably liberal
credentials and her African-American heritage. In some ways, the
Jordan Commission's report provided cover for restrictionists who did
not have to fear as much the usual charges of xenophobia. President
Bill Clinton, eager to pander to voters in a presidential election year,
heartily approved of the commission's recommendations. The Republican presidential nominee, Bob Dole, feeling a need to assuage Pat
Buchanan and the populist wing of the GOP, also endorsed the Jordan
Commission's proposals.

With the two presidential candidates, the chairs of the immigration
subcommittees, the prestigious Commission on Immigration Reform,
and the general public all supporting reductions, it appeared all but
certain that the United States would enact a restrictionist measure for
the first time since 1924. But that did not happen. All proposals on
legal immigration were scuttled by the end of the 104th Congress. How
and why did this happen?

What happened in 1996 was not so much different from what has
occurred regularly since 1965: Restrictionists, who had successfully
lobbied to limit immigration in the past, have been routed by immigration enthusiasts in recent decades. In 1990, for example, a modestly
restrictionist bill was transformed into a bill that increased immigration

by 40%—thanks to the shrewd maneuverings of proimmigration activists. Since the 1960s, an unusual but powerful coalition between the "Right" (as represented by business and free-market Republican ideologues) and the "Left" (as represented by ethnic lobbyists, religious/humanitarian organizations, and Democratic politicians) has managed to defeat restrictionist proposals. Though these two sides have wholly different reasons for supporting high levels of immigration, both the Right and the Left have found it mutually beneficial to work together and have dominated the immigration policy arena.

Alexis de Tocqueville noted in 1835 in his book *Democracy in America* that, "In no country in the world has the principle of association been more successfully used or applied to a greater multitude of objects than in America." That keen observation, like so many of Tocqueville's incisive commentaries, still holds true today: the "principle of association" best explains American public policy. Over the years, political scientists like David Truman and Robert Dahl have elaborated on Tocqueville's assessment of the primacy of groups in American politics. Their pluralist framework of various interest groups competing against one another most aptly describes the immigration policy process today. This does not necessarily mean that other theories are completely invalid; elite concern for business and the state's foreign policy prerogative are partially responsible for America's generous policy. But they explain only parts of the puzzle. A modified pluralist theory most comprehensively explains the divergence between public opinion and public policy on immigration: conservative and liberal interest groups, ranging from ethnic lobbies to businesses, have worked together to maintain high levels of immigration, despite opposition from the mass public.[3]

Two major fortuitous historical circumstances were responsible for the change in the power distribution between the restrictionists and the proimmigrationists. The first was the ascendancy of conservative economics in the late 1970s, an era of rapid globalization. The emphasis on laissez-faire policies was conducive to high levels of immigration because free-market ideologues wanted people, like capital, to flow freely among countries. Although the doctrinaire laissez-faire heydays of the Reagan era are over, neoclassical economic theory still has considerable influence among policymakers today. That a Democratic president would support the North American Free Trade Agreement (NAFTA) and the General Agreement on Trade and Tariffs (GATT) over the protests of labor unions is a testament to the regnant free market spirit in a globalized economy. The power of ideas should never be doubted.[4] As Skip Garling of the restrictionist Federation of American Immigration Reform points out, "Political and ideological persuasion plays a big role in determining [the legislators'] views."[5]

Second, the civil rights zeitgeist eroded the power of nativist groups that had historically played a prominent role in restricting immigration. The restrictionist bloc, which had considerable clout in the early twentieth century, found itself losing political power vis-à-vis the proimmigrationists. These two historical changes facilitated the unusual alliance between the Right and the Left. Many Republicans supported immigration as a way to aid businesses and to reaffirm their belief in the free market, and the Left was able to fight successfully for high levels of immigration because demagogic racial appeals no longer had the power they once had.

It is important to stress that ideology—whether it be laissez-faire, liberal humanitarianism, or cultural traditionalism—plays the most prominent role for legislators representing districts or states with a sparse immigrant population. As Senator Alan Simpson admits, "I represented Wyoming so there was less constituent pressure compared to other [senators]."[6] Political reality, however, can temper and often overshadow ideology in many cases. The vast majority of immigrants reside in six states: California, New York, Texas, Florida, New Jersey, and Illinois. And immigrants are further concentrated in certain (mainly urban) areas of those states. So, for example, a congressman in districts with a high foreign-born population (such as Los Angeles) may feel intense political pressure to vote against restrictionist legislation, lest he appear nativist and alienate his many foreign-born constituents.

The concentration of immigrants in certain areas also means that the costs of immigration are unevenly distributed in a federal system like ours. Immigrants usually pay most of their taxes to the federal government, but they use state-funded social programs the most. Fiscal costs of immigration for, say, Wyoming, will be far less than for California. A RAND Corporation study recently reported that each California household headed by a native-born American had a $1,178 tax burden for immigrants' use of state public services, while citizens of most other states enjoyed a net tax gain.[7] Public education is primarily locally funded with minimal federal aid, so the residents near high-immigrant areas end up paying for this cost. And to a lesser extent, they also have to bear the burden of health care costs and other social services provided by the state government to immigrants. Thus, even an ideologically laissez-faire representative from Orange County—a district near Los Angeles but with a smaller foreign-born population—might face political pressure to espouse restrictionist views because (1) he does not have to worry as much about appearing anti-immigrant in his district but (2) his constituents will still have to pay higher local taxes for the education of nearby immigrants' children and bear the costs of more state government spending for immigrants. How a representative will vote is not an exact science, but, on the whole, representatives from areas with few immigrants will have more latitude in determining their attitude toward immigration. These legislators are more susceptible to ideological persuasion because they have relatively less constituent pressure. They may have a position based on ideology or instinct (e.g., immigrants are good for businesses), although electoral pressures should never be totally discounted. The fate of immigration bills thus often depends on how these legislators from low-immigrant areas vote.

THE RISE OF THE RIGHT: MALAISE OF THE SEVENTIES AND THE FREE MARKET GOSPEL

From the end of World War II until 1974, the United States enjoyed unparalleled economic growth and stood as the hegemonic economic power in the world. Virtually every single economic indicator was positive during this period. Family income rose, inflation and unemployment remained low, and the Gross National Product (GNP) grew at a robust rate. Millions of Americans bought their first home and enjoyed comfortable middle-class lives: automobiles, televisions, and other material amenities found their way into their homes. Opportunities seemed endless. The ever-expanding economic pie even allowed business and labor to have an implicit agreement of accommodation during this period: labor would not agitate business as long as economic growth continued and wages for workers increased. The 1965 Immigration Act passed without much controversy or protest from the usual quarters (such as organized labor) in part because of the vibrant economy.

By the late 1970s, the United States was mired in economic doldrums and its superpower status was being severely challenged in a rapidly globalizing economy. The trusty postwar Keynesian formula for economic growth no longer worked. The country suffered from sluggish growth and inordinately high interest rates. From 1950 to 1973, the GNP grew nearly 4% a year; but during the 1970s and early 1980s, the GNP growth averaged an anemic 1.6% annually, and there were four years when there were actual declines in the real GNP.[8] There was also high unemployment and double-digit inflation. This was not supposed to happen. The Phillips Curve stated that if unemployment was high, a little inflation would solve it; conversely, a little inflation would be cured by unemployment. Mysteriously, though, both high unemployment and high inflation persisted. Economists even created a new term, "stagflation," to describe this high-inflation, slow-growth economy. Inflation was so out of control that a Republican president, Richard Nixon, instituted price and wage controls. A year before its enactment, Nixon's Council of Economic Advisers had argued that, "Short of an emergency of kind which does not exist, mandatory comprehensive price and wage controls are undesirable, unnecessary and probably unworkable."[9] Apparently, by Friday the 13th of August 1971, there was such an emergency. President Nixon met with his advisers—who included John Connally, George Shultz, Peter Peterson, Paul McCracken, Arthur Burns, Herbert Stein, Paul Volcker, and William Safire—at Camp David on that day and decided to enact price and wage controls. The United States' economic woes were so baffling that Nixon's successor, Gerald Ford, even comedically wore WIN buttons (for "Whip Inflation Now"). Jimmy Carter did no better, as slow growth, high unemployment, and double-digit inflation doomed his presidency.

If stagflation wasn't bad enough, the United States' economic power eroded relative to that of Japan and Germany. As exports flooded the United States, American companies found it harder to compete against foreign companies. America's percentage of the world's GNP slowly but steadily declined. Chrysler's flirtation with bankruptcy confirmed many Americans' suspicion that the United States had lost its edge in the global economy. While Japanese automobile manufacturers like Honda and Toyota enjoyed a rapidly growing market share, American carmakers were producing large clunkers. And Japanese television and VCRs—originally American inventions—virtually dominated the American market. The United States appeared to be on the slow but inexorable path of decline.

Moribund liberals had no politically palatable answers. Under this cloud of pessimism and discontent, conservative economics offered a ray of hope. Conservatives blamed high taxes, excessive government spending, and onerous government regulations for America's woes. The solution to this malaise was a return to free-market principles in the form of "supply-side economics," which stressed the importance of incentives and deregulation. Arthur Laffer, Robert Mundell, and a handful of other academics, spearheaded the supply-side movement intellectually. The supply-side gospel was then spread by savvy publicists such as Jude Wanniski (who now advises Jack Kemp) and journalists like Robert Bartley, who did a magnificent job in selling supply-side economics to conservative politicians and eventually to the American public. This supply-side panacea was reinforced by the manic logic of a globalizing economy: to remain competitive with other nations, the United States must keep in check burdensome regulations and high taxation.

Most of the intellectual ferment during this time period occurred on the Right. Scores of books eulogizing laissez-faire were published during the late 1970s and early 1980s: among them were Jude Wanniski's *The Way the World Works*, George Gilder's *Wealth and Poverty*, and Irving Kristol's *Two Cheers for Capitalism*. Publications like *The Public Interest* and the newly reincarnated *Commentary* espoused supply-side economics as the antidote to the country's relative economic decline. The *Wall Street Journal* played an especially important role in providing a forum for these free-market ideas. And conservative think tanks, such as the American Enterprise Institute, the Heritage Foundation, the Cato Institute, and the Hudson Institute, produced copious amounts of research. Ultimately, Republicans like Representative Jack Kemp and President Ronald Reagan, along with a handful of loyal Republicans and conservative Democrats, translated these ideas into policy.

The rise of this conservative economics coincided with the increase in legal immigration. Though many people were perturbed by the increase in immigration during a time of sluggish economic growth, many conservatives took a more sanguine view. Laissez-faire ideology viewed restrictions on immigration as another form of inefficient and pernicious government regulation. Right-wing ideologues thought that people should move freely in a competitive global economy; an open immigration policy was concomitant to free trade. An influx of immigrants could make America more competitive by attracting the best and the brightest people around the world into the United States.

Conservatives preferred an immigration system based more on skills than on family connection, but they nevertheless accepted family-based immigration as economically beneficial. Supply-side guru George Gilder in his best-selling book *Wealth and Poverty* boldly wrote, "Unless we wish to adopt an immoral and economically self-destructive policy of prohibiting immigration, there will be poverty in America for centuries to come."[10] According to Gilder, "Few of these entrepreneurial feats would have happened without the crucial contributions of labor, ingenuity, and industrial daring of a new generation of immigrants."[11] The *Wall Street Journal* editorial page went even so far as to suggest a constitutional amendment that would declare open borders. Other commentators chronicled the entrepreneurial spirit of immigrants and cited examples of hi-tech companies like Sun Microsystems and AST computers that were founded by immigrants.

These pundits also saw the children of immigrants in a global context. In recent decades, scores of studies have reported on the decline in math and science test scores and the fraying work ethic among American students. One bright spot amid these somber stories was the academic achievement of Asian students, most of whom were immigrants or children of immigrants. These students in the future could lead America in the hi-tech fields against countries like Japan and Germany, said the proimmigration pundits. Conservative columnist George Will, for example, wrote that "America needs more university students like Asian-Americans" at a time when there is "high anxiety about declining educational standards and rising competition from abroad, and especially from the Pacific Rim."[12] This idea of immigration fueling America in a global economy permeated to the mass public: *Time* magazine devoted a front-cover story in 1987 entitled, "The New Whiz Kids: Why Asian Americans Are Doing So Well."[13]

Think tanks played a crucial role in providing the ammunition in the battle of ideas. Virtually all the prominent Right-leaning think tanks—from the libertarian Cato Institute to the staunchly conservative Heritage Foundation—concurred that immigrants were an economic boon to the United States. These new conservatives were very ideological in their animus against government regulations—more so than Republicans from previous eras. A moderately rightward-leaning Harvard economist recently summed up the conservative case for immigration: "If we have a market for butter, why not also a market for visas?"[14]

The GOP being a relatively probusiness party, many of its members obviously have a political stake in providing needed immigrants to businesses. Businesses devoted most of their lobbying efforts toward increasing skills-based visas and reforming the labor certification process for temporary workers. Republicans catered to their demands by tripling the number of skills-based visas to 140,000 in 1990 and then, in 1996, buckling under political pressure to scrap proposals that imposed regulations on business-oriented immigration visas. Most businesses were neutral on family-reunification immigration. If they did comment on it, it was in relation to business-related visas. As Austin T.

Fragomen of the American Council on International Personnel told Congress, "Although the bill proposes extensive changes in the area of family-based immigrants, ACIP will only comment upon provisions of direct concern to this business community. . . . [But] often a multinational executive or manager will reject a career opportunity in a country whose immigration laws disallow [family] members to accompany or join the employee."[15]

Though Republicans—as well as many Democrats—supported skills-based immigration to aid small businesses in their districts as well as large corporations that contribute campaign donations, it would be a mistake to ascribe only political motivation for their interest in immigration. A large minority of Republicans support family-based immigration, though it might not have direct political consequence for the business community. Ideology plays an important role in shaping many Republicans' views on immigration.

Republicans are split into two camps on the issue of immigration. Traditionalists who worry about the cultural impact of immigration and those representatives from states accepting high numbers of immigrants (like Representative Lamar Smith of Texas) tend to vote more along restrictionist lines. A slim majority of Republicans fall under this traditionalist/restrictionist camp, which dates back to the first "conservative" party, the Federalists. On the other side, there is a large minority of staunch free-market Republicans who support high levels of immigration, including family-based visas, because it is consonant with their ideology. For example, Representatives Dick Chrysler (R-Mich.) and Sam Brownback (R-Kans.), who were members of the ideological 1994 Republican freshmen class, scuttled legal immigration reform in 1996 through their "killer" amendment. And Majority Whip Dick Armey, one of the more zealous free-market conservatives in Congress, supports high levels of immigration. "Should we reduce legal immigration? I'm hard-pressed to think of a single problem that would be solved by shutting off the supply of willing and eager new Americans," he said.[16] Also, both Jack Kemp and Steve Forbes, the two leading supply-side gurus, have declared their support for a generous immigration policy. "America would not be the high-tech leader if we didn't have legal immigration," explained Steve Forbes during the 1996 primary season. "Just go to those laboratories. One-fourth to one-half of those Ph.D.s are foreign-born. They're contributing to America."[17]

It wasn't only the free market ideologues who viewed immigration in a global context. Congressional witnesses—from businesses to academia to ethnic groups—spoke of the importance of a generous and flexible immigration policy in a competitive economy. William E. Kirwan, the president of the University of Maryland, explained, "The subject of global interdependence that we hear educators, business and government leaders discussing so often today is nowhere more evident than in academia, where the development and exchange of knowledge is increasingly an international enterprise. Ideas and learning know no national boundaries. . . . Maintaining excellence and leadership in our academic programs is particularly important at a time when the United States faces growing competition from other nations in economic and scientific fields."[18] The Chamber of Commerce, though it was specifically lobbying for skills-based visas, nevertheless spoke of competition in a broader sense: "[Immigration] barriers inhibit the flexibility of U.S. companies with overseas operations and severely restrict America's ability to compete in a global economy."[19] Ethnic groups also stressed the competition theme. Raul Yzaguirre of the National Council of La Raza said, "Immigrants keep some U.S. industries competitive by increasing returns to capital."[20]

Thus, the United States' relative economic decline in the 1970s in a rapidly globalizing economy played an important role in building support for immigration among Republicans. Though Keynesian economics said little specifically about immigration, its demise paved the way for the neoclassical economics that still reigns today. Many Republicans had always supported skills-based immigration as a favor to businesses, but the ascendancy of conservative economics convinced a large contingent of free-market ideologues in Congress of the benefits of immigration in general.

THE LEFT: RACIAL LIBERALISM AND IMMIGRATION

During the 1960s, Americans had to confront the wrenching issue of racial equality as blacks began to demand equal political rights and an opportunity to partake in the American dream. Lunch table sit-ins, marches, and other forms of peaceful protests earned the sympathy of many Americans. The indelible television images of racial demagogues like George Wallace blocking the entrance to the University of Alabama and of "Bull" Connor bludgeoning peaceful black protesters ultimately helped spell the doom for legalized segregation. After much turmoil and bloodshed, the civil rights movement succeeded in passing the Civil

Rights Act of 1964 and the Voting Rights Act of 1965. More impor-
tantly, the civil rights zeitgeist changed the racial attitudes of many
Americans. Racial tolerance became a virtue appreciated by a majority
of Americans: very few Americans today will openly espouse racist
views, lest they be ostracized.

The impact of the civil rights movement seeped into immigration
policy. Ethnocentric arguments had historically played a prominent role
in limiting immigration, especially from Eastern and Southern Europe
and Asia. Restrictionists argued that newer immigrants were morally
and intellectually inferior and could not assimilate into the American
culture. When Congress held hearings in 1920, numerous interest
groups, ranging from the American Legion to labor unions, testified
against immigration, using overtly racist arguments. One witness argued that, "It is their [the Japanese] misfortune that they do not
assimilate or blend with our peoples. It means mongrelization and
degeneracy."[21] And there were scores of lobbying groups dedicated
solely to limiting immigration. Among them were the California Ori-
ental Exclusion League, the Anti-Asiatic Exclusion League, the Immigration Restriction League, the Anti-Japanese League, the Native Sons
of the Golden West, and the Eugenics Research Association. These
groups were unrepentant in candidly expressing their racial outlook.
"The character of a nation is determined primarily by its racial qualities;
that is, by the hereditary physical, mental, and moral or temperamental
traits of its people," said Harry H. Laughlin of the Eugenics Research
Association, in explaining his support for immigration limitations.[22]

When Congress considered the Walter-McCarran Act in 1952,
overtly racist arguments were already becoming less socially acceptable.
Despite maintaining a national origins quota in this act, Congress
denied any racial motivation. "Without giving any credence to any
theory of Nordic superiority, the Committee believes that the adoption
of the national origins quota formula was rational and logical," com-
mented the Judiciary Committee.[23]

By the 1960s, as the civil rights movement gained larger acceptance
among the general public, most Americans at least publicly eschewed
racial arguments. The civil rights movement had created a political
climate conducive to immigration reform. The debate over the 1965
Immigration Act showed the direct link between civil rights and
immigration. Attorney General Robert Kennedy testified, "Every-
where else in our national life, we have eliminated discrimination based
on national origins. Yet this system [of discrimination] is still the

foundation of our immigration law."[24] One congressman argued, "[J]ust as we sought to eliminate discrimination in our land through the Civil Rights act, today we seek by phasing out the national origins quota system to eliminate discrimination in immigration to this nation composed of the descendants of immigrants."[25]

Ever since, the concept of racial equality—though maybe not fully realized in terms of tangible results—has firmly established itself in the American polity. Whenever Congress considers bills limiting immigration, legislators defensively deny that they are motivated by racism. "It's not nativist, not racist, not mean," was a popular refrain used by Senator Alan Simpson in describing his bills.[26] The most salient example of how racial attitudes had changed the politics of immigration was the debate over the "diversity" program in the 1990 act for underrepresented nations adversely affected by the 1965 act. The House Judiciary Committee justified the program by arguing that, "The Committee is convinced that in order to correct ongoing inequities in current law, changes must be made to further enhance and promote diversity within the present system."[27] Seventy years earlier, policymakers used blatantly racist arguments to justify an exclusive Western European immigration system. In 1990, legislators were using the rhetoric of affirmative action—with its emphasis on past discrimination, diversity, and underrepresentation—to establish a modest 55,000 diversity program for Europeans.

Most important, most nativist groups had disappeared by the end of the 1960s. Just as the membership of the White Citizens' Alliance declined in the South, so did the Immigration Restrictionist League and the Anti-Asiatic Exclusion League in the immigration policy network. Whatever nativist organizations still remained were cast off as fringe groups and no longer taken seriously by Congress. In the dozens of hearings that Congress has held on immigration since 1965, not one nativist group has testified. The only major national group solely dedicated to limiting immigration today is the Federation for American Immigration Reform (FAIR).[28] This disappearance of a powerful bloc greatly eroded the political influence of restrictionists.

The civil rights zeitgeist not only weakened restrictionists but it also empowered ethnic groups that have a stake in increased immigration. "Ethnic organizations gain their future political power by having as many immigrants [as possible] in the country, so they can tell [ethnic minorities] that they would have never gotten here without their help," argues former Senator Alan Simpson.[29] That view might be overly cynical, but it is true that ethnic groups began to play a more prominent role in immigration policy starting in the 1960s when immigration expanded. And as working-class whites began to flee the Democratic Party in the late 1960s, racial minorities became a crucial bloc of the liberal coalition. Among the more influential ethnic groups in the immigration policy network are the National Council of La Raza, the Organization of Chinese Americans, the American Jewish Committee, the American Committee on Italian Migration, the National Asian Pacific American Legal Consortium, and the Mexican American Legal Defense Fund. These groups are not afraid to express their displeasure. For instance, many of the Hispanic and Asian delegates demonstrated their opposition to the Simpson-Mazzoli bill—which had the support of many Democrats—by protesting and threatening to boycott at the Democratic National Convention. "Simpson-Mazzoli wasn't passed by magic," said California delegate Maria Ochoa. "It was passed with the help of Democrats and we don't like that."[30]

ACT I: "AN ABSOLUTE, DELIBERATE EFFORT"

When Congress began considering legal immigration reform in the late 1980s, it did not initially seem that an ardently proimmigration bill would result. The Select Commission on Immigration and Refugee Policy in 1981 had recommended a moderate increase in legal immigration to ease family-reunification backlogs, on the hopeful condition that illegal immigration would abate after the passage of employer sanctions—for a net neutral movement in immigration numbers. Initial statistics seemed to suggest that the 1986 Immigration Reform and Control Act was working. The INS reported that border apprehensions had fallen from an all-time high of 1,767,400 in 1986 to 954,243 in 1989.[31] Later studies contested the IRCA's efficacy on two main grounds: (1) illegal immigration began to increase again after 1989; and (2) decreased funding for Border Patrol had led to fewer border apprehensions during the late 1980s. But perceptions, not reality, matter more in public policy. The Immigration Reform and Control Act had seemingly stemmed the tide of illegal aliens, and so Congress thought it could accommodate a slight increase in legal immigrants. But there was no burning demand for a massive 40% increase in immigration as the final version of the bill allowed.

In 1988, Senators Alan Simpson and Edward Kennedy, the two ranking members of the immigration subcommittee, drafted a bill that set a total annual cap of 590,000, which, for the first time ever, included immediate relatives of American citizens. Immediate relatives would still be numerically exempt, but they would come at the expense of other family-preference immigrants. The bill also established a separate, "independent" visa system for people without families residing in the United States. This 590,000 cap could be considered modestly restrictionist: it expanded annual quotas but set a firmer ceiling to prevent future unexpected increases in immigration. But when the final bill was signed by President Bush, it was decisively proimmigration: it increased immigration to 675,000 without setting a firm cap. A very informal but potent Left-Right coalition was responsible for this surprising outcome.

By the late 1970s—when the impact of the 1965 immigration act was finally being felt—the Left and the Right began to see eye-to-eye on the issue of immigration. Ethnic groups pressured Democrats to defend family-based and diversity immigration, while businesses prodded Republicans to expand skills-based immigration. Businesses had little interest in family-based immigration, but they did not oppose it, either. Conversely, ethnic groups' main concern was family-based immigration, but they were willing to tolerate skills-based immigration. Both parties also had ideological reasons for supporting immigration. The Left's liberal, multicultural humanitarianism and the Right's laissez-faire proclivities meshed well with a generous immigration policy. Previously, the two sides had not worked with each other much on any issues; their differences in ideologies and interests were usually too vast. But in 1990, the Right and the Left realized that they shared mutual interests and could succeed if they worked together instead of fighting against each other.

This Left-Right coalition worked spectacularly in the 1990 Immigration Act. Businesses and ethnic groups realized that it did not have to be a zero-sum game—that is, family-based visas did not have to come at the expense of business skills-based visas, or vice versa. They could pursue a "logrolling" strategy to have both family-based and skills-based visas.[32] The Organization of Chinese Americans, for example, stated that it "endorses the concepts of employment-sponsored and independent [diversity] immigration, but NOT at the expense of family-sponsored immigration. It is possible . . . to develop a formula that enables increases in these three areas."[33] Businesses returned the favor to ethnic groups. According to Congressman Lamar Smith, "Their [the businesses] hearts were in the employment-based visas, but some supported family-based immigration to join forces in a coalition."[34]

This informal Left-Right coalition was primarily orchestrated by Rick Swartz, a D.C.-based political entrepreneur and immigration lobbyist. A self-described liberal and a civil rights lawyer, Swartz began his involvement in immigration in the 1970s when he fought on behalf of Haitian refugees and against the English-only movement. In 1981, he established the National Immigration Forum, an umbrella organization for various proimmigration groups, which he headed for several years. And true to his coalition politics, the liberal Swartz received financial support from Richard Gilder, a conservative Wall Street businessman who supports free trade and generous immigration and has given financial support to pro-growth Republicans like Jack Kemp.[35]

Swartz carefully coordinated the activities between the Right and Left. Early 1990 strategy memos indicated that, "A primary tactic shall be influencing points of decision by framing the terms of a bipartisan (when possible) resolution of issues through the intelligentsia, constituencies, the Congress and the Executive," and that, "there are opportunities to find common ground between liberal and conservative thinkers who believe in the value of immigration."[36]

On the Right, Swartz worked closely with business lobbyists who wanted to increase skills-based visas. Business groups lobbied Congress to expand skills-based visas from 54,000 to 140,000. There was a deliberate strategy to appeal to Republicans' laissez-faire leanings. "Frame the affirmative value of immigrants to America's international competitiveness," advised one strategy memo.[37] Business groups accordingly did so. Daryl Buffenstein of the Chamber of Commerce said that current "immigration laws are a barrier to trade and investment, that they inhibit the efficiency and flexibility of U.S. companies trading and operating abroad, and that they substantially increase the costs of conducting international business."[38] Top business groups used this argument in lobbying congressmen.

In addition to the direct, "inside" lobbying of legislators, there was an effort to shape the public opinion on immigration, primarily through the media. Swartz, for example, set up a meeting with the editorial writers of the *Wall Street Journal* to convince them to provide favorable coverage for the immigration bill.[39] The influential and widely circulated newspaper complied, devoting a positive editorial to the immigration bill during the crucial conference agreement period in October. Conservative think tanks were also busy at work pushing for increased immigration. The Cato Institute and the Alexis de Tocqueville Institute disseminated proimmigration op-ed pieces and studies to various newspapers and journals. The pieces stressed the economic virtues of immigration in hopes of garnering public support as well as Republican legislators' votes.

What possibly helped business the most was a bipartisan consensus at the time that the United States would have a skilled labor shortage in the future. Even the Labor Department, which is not traditionally known for its proimmigration views, testified that the United States would need skilled labor in the future.[40] And the Hudson Institute issued a very influential report, *Workforce 2000*, that popularized the notion that the United States would suffer from labor shortages in the future and needed an influx of skilled labor. Both Republicans and Democrats generally agreed that skills-based immigration should be increased to help rectify this impending "problem."

Instrumental to solidifying the Right side of the Left-Right coalition was swaying the Bush White House to support increased immigration. Though the Bush administration was not active in crafting the 1990 act, proimmigrationists feared that it could still scuttle the bill by vetoing it or indirectly influencing the positions of Republican legislators. Indeed, the Bush Justice Department and the Immigration and Naturalization Services publicly had said that they did not want to increase family-based immigration. Swartz worked to change the Bush administration's stance by finding a sympathetic ear in Charles Kolb, the deputy domestic adviser to President Bush. "He was new to the job and was looking for a couple of issues to hang his hat on, and immigration became one of them," explains Swartz. "He was a critical player in turning the Bush White House from being captive to the anti-immigrant Justice Department and the INS, and into proimmigration. He was persuaded that the left-right coalition was the way that the Bush White House could come out a winner."[41] In time, Kolb convinced the Bush administration to become more receptive to a liberal immigration reform and to pursue a logrolling strategy that appeased interest groups from the Left and the Right. This won the support of many Republican congressmen who were reluctant to cross their president.

Just as important as winning support from Republican congressmen was convincing Senator Edward Kennedy to become more supportive of family-based immigration. Kennedy, the primary author of the 1965 immigration act, has long served as the liberal standard-bearer on immigration: most legislators do not know the nuances of immigration law, but if Kennedy says it's okay, then other liberals, who may not be as knowledgeable on immigration, dutifully follow. Kennedy and Simpson had a very good working relationship, and they had coauthored the original Senate bill with a firm immigration ceiling in it. Swartz pursued a deliberate strategy of creating wedges between Simpson and Kennedy. By making the Bush administration more proimmigration, it forced Kennedy to become more proimmigration and steer away from Simpson's more restrictive views. "It's hard for Kennedy to appear less proimmigration than a Republican White House," points out Swartz. "So by making the Bush White House more proimmigration, we could then tell Edward Kennedy, 'Are you going to let George Bush be more proimmigrant than you, given the great tradition of the Kennedy family?' " (Interview with author, April 2, 1997). That wedge strategy seemed to work: Kennedy became more receptive to increased immigration as the congressional session went on.

The traditionally liberal ethnic and religious groups were active in their lobbying efforts as well. The Organization of Chinese Americans, for example, employed both inside and outside lobbying strategies to get their way. In addition to lobbying vacillating members of the Judiciary committees, the OCA tried to galvanize the Asian community into sending letters to their congressmen. "We did a lot of media work with press releases and tried to reach out to the Asian community through the Chinese and ethnic media," says Daphne Kwok of the Organization of Chinese Americans.[42] Other ethnic groups also engaged in a direct mail campaign targeted toward key congressmen. The impact of such mail campaigns cannot be underestimated: congressional staffers assiduously keep track of letters as an important barometer of constituent opinion on important legislation. All congressmen consider reelection to be paramount, so they pay very close attention to constituent mail because those people are the ones who will likely vote in the next election.

Swartz emphasizes that he made an "absolutely deliberate effort" to avoid zero-sum politics: he made sure that businesses and ethnic groups did not try to compete against each other for a finite pie of visas.[43] Both could get what they wanted if they stuck together and played their cards right. Ethnic groups also avoided zero-sum politics among themselves. Asian and Latino groups supported family-based immigration, while European ethnics like the Irish supported the establishment of an independent diversity program (because they do not have the family connections that Asians and Latinos have). Instead of competing against each other, they agreed to expand immigration in all areas. As Donald Martin of the Irish Immigration Reform Movement told Congressman Howard Berman (D-Calif.), "The Irish Immigration Reform Movement sees dealing with the issues of diversity as an additive process. In other words, we don't seek to attack the family preference system. Our grievance against the family preference system is that we are not in it and we won't be in it without the Congress helping us."[44]

Ethnic groups found a very sympathetic voice in Bruce A. Morrison (D-Conn.). He replaced the more conservative Romano Mazzoli (D-Ky.) as the head of the Immigration, Refugees and International Law Subcommittee when the House considered immigration reform in 1990. Morrison was then involved in a contentious Democratic primary for the Connecticut governorship against an opponent with the surname O'Brien. Morrison decided not to step on any toes of powerful interest groups (like the large Irish Catholic population in Connecticut) by being restrictive and opted instead to write a very generous bill to woo votes in a logrolling fashion.[45] His bill would have increased immigration by a whopping 60% to 800,000 annual visas, which included special diversity visas that would disproportionately help the Irish. And as time ran out in the 101st Congress, the conferees decided to split the difference between the Senate's 630,000 ceiling with the House's 800,000 limit for a total of 675,000.

This informal Left-Right coalition proved potent. Both Republicans and Democrats felt the political pressure to vote for the bill and award all the interest groups involved. The Senate approved the bill 89–8, while the House voted in favor 264–118. The House Republicans voted in favor 93–64, while Democrats voted 171–54. The high number of votes from Democrats was expected as liberals are dependable supporters of high immigration and ethnic groups. Key to the passage of the bill was wooing the support of Republicans, especially on restrictive floor amendments.[46] A cadre of free-market Republicans defected from most members of their party by voting against amendments that would have killed the bill. Swartz later noted that the proimmigrationists' success was attributable to "our success in persuading 50 pro-growth Republicans led by Vin Weber and Hamilton Fish to support significant immigration increases despite the opposition from the Justice Department. It was also significant that business groups with which I work helped us on these amendment votes."[47]

ACT II: "WE NEED TO HANG TOGETHER OR BE HUNG TOGETHER"

As in 1990, the same informal Left-Right coalition worked to defend immigration in 1996.[48] By 1995, the political climate had changed, and anti-immigration fever had hit its peak. Only a year before—the year of the "Angry White Male," as it was dubbed by the media—Proposition 187, the anti-illegal-immigration initiative, passed overwhelmingly in California. Legal immigration reform seemed to be next: polls showed that nearly two-thirds of Americans wanted to curtail immigration. Even among policymakers, there seemed to be a restrictionist consensus. In the now Republican-controlled Congress, Representative Lamar Smith and Senator Alan Simpson, both restrictionists, held the chairs for the immigration subcommittees and planned to introduce their own immigration bills.

Both the Left and the Right were worried. Ethnic groups wanted to protect family-based visas and the diversity program, while businesses feared reductions in skills-based immigration and more onerous regulations on temporary workers. Both groups' fears were realized. Representative Smith was the first to take action. He introduced a bill (HR 1915, later renamed HR 2202) that curtailed legal immigration by a third. It reduced family-based immigration from 480,000 to 330,000 primarily by eliminating visas for siblings and adult children of citizens as well as permanent residents, abolishing the diversity program, and including immediate relatives under the 330,000 cap. On the business side, the bill slightly cut skills-based visas from 140,000 to 135,000 and imposed stricter requirements for employers sponsoring immigrant workers. The bill also included an illegal immigration component with provisions for stronger border enforcement and expedited deportation procedures. Representative Smith began debate on his immigration bill in the House Judiciary Subcommittee on Immigration and Claim in July 1995, and he managed to maintain enough party discipline in the small subcommittee to steer his bill relatively unscathed out of the subcommittee.

Once the bill went to the full Judiciary Committee in October of 1995, it began to face stiffer resistance from interest groups. Ethnic groups and businesses criticized the bill, and Rick Swartz tried to orchestrate the same Left-Right coalition that had proved so successful in 1990. This time around, Swartz was aided by Grover Norquist, the head of the libertarian Americans for Tax Reform. Norquist, an old friend and unofficial adviser to Newt Gingrich, specializes in creating coalitions among different conservative factions. He holds morning meetings every Wednesday of what he dubs the "Leave Us Alone Coalition," which includes disparate groups like the National Rifle Association, the Christian Coalition, and the Cato Institute.

On the advice of the libertarian Cato Institute economist Stephen Moore, Swartz decided to pursue a strategy of splitting the bill into legal and illegal immigration parts. Proimmigrationists hoped to derail legal immigration reform by diverting Congress's attention to the more politically popular issue of illegal immigrants, who do not have the same interest group backing as legal immigrants. Representative Smith vehemently opposed splitting the bills. "The people who supported splitting legal and illegal immigration argued that they didn't oppose reform. They only wanted to consider them separately—or at least that's what they said. But my point was that splitting is killing it," Smith recalls.[49] And he was right: As Daphne Kwok of the Organization of Chinese Americans candidly admits, "The strategy was to split the bill, hoping that legal immigration would die because time was running out."[50]

Businesses, however, were lukewarm to the Left-Right coalition this time around. "Split the bill effort did not automatically or easily attract the support and confidence of the business community," says Swartz. "Smith's bill in the House side was very modest when it came to restrictions on business visas, though he went after family-based visas with an ax."[51] Representative Smith, fearing that a Left-Right coalition would thwart his immigration bill, took no chances. Just before the Judiciary Committee vote, he agreed to remove all restrictions on business-based visas. In return, many business groups, despite howls of protests from the left-wing of the coalition, agreed not to lobby for the "split-the-bill amendment" that was being offered in committee. The Left-Right coalition that had worked so beautifully in 1990 seemed to have been torn asunder by Smith's shrewd tactic. One high-tech lobbyist explained why he ended up siding with Smith:

> We looked at this split-the-bill alliance and decided it was just too fragile to stay together for the long term. I heard people say, "I can't go to my CEO and say, 'We're not taking Smith's deal because we're working with these family and ethnic groups.'" Plus, we weren't sure those guys would be with us in the end, anyway. When people started screaming about businesses importing immigrants as cheap labor, maybe they'd join in and we'd get screwed. It was just a clash of cultures.[52]

Swartz, to no avail, advised business lobbyists to oppose the bill: "I told them it was suicidal. We have to hang together or be hung together."[53] Business groups, however, took Representative Smith's offer and opposed the split-the-bill amendment. Assured of business support, all but one Republican voted against this amendment, and the bill left the committee with both the legal and illegal immigration components intact.

Action now moved to the Senate. Emboldened by the House's success, Senator Alan Simpson introduced his own immigration bill. Like the House bill, Simpson's bill proposed reducing legal immigration by a third. But Simpson made a colossal political blunder by advocating draconian changes in business immigration: he would have reduced skills-based visas from 140,000 to 90,000 and imposed a fee of $10,000 or 10% of the employee's yearly compensation—whichever was greater—for each immigrant worker brought to the United States.[54]

Businesses were shocked and outraged by Simpson's provisions. "We'd like it stopped dead," said Phyllis Eisen of the National Association of Manufacturers.[55] Added Ira Rubenstein, a lawyer for Microsoft: "It was like the end of the world. It was as if the contributions of immigrants to high-tech firms had never occurred. As if [Intel president] Andy Grove never existed. As if the huge percentage of foreign students in U.S. graduate programs had been waved away. As if the realities of our whole business had been completely ignored and what was left was the ideology of restriction."[56] Swartz explains, "Simpson emasculated the business side as well as the family side. That sort of got them [businesses] back thinking that, 'Geez, split-the-bill [strategy] looks attractive now that Simpson is going after us like crazy. Maybe we're going to have to rejoin forces with ethnic groups and churches in this strange, unusual alliance.' "[57] At about this time, Labor Secretary Robert Reich and Senator Edward Kennedy expressed support for the changes, further alarming business lobbyists and pushing them into vigorously fighting these restrictions. "Bill Gates allied [himself] with those cats at Cato and Grover Norquist . . . and [Gates] went crazy, saying that he would never be able to invent a new piece of software," recalls Simpson.[58] Rankled by this business pressure, Simpson decided to follow the way of Representative Smith, and he voluntarily offered to drop his provisions on business-based visas during the Senate Judiciary mark-ups. "Business was confronted with a choice: Do they trust Simpson? Was [his word] going to be sufficient? Or were they running risks now that we knew his true attitudes? Instead of cutting a deal with

Simpson, they came back to the coalition," explains Swartz (Interview with author, April 2, 1997). And the fact that Labor Secretary Reich and Senator Kennedy had come out against employment-based immigration scared businesses: they faced a potential coalition of restrictionist conservatives like Simpson and prolabor liberals, which would fight employment-based immigration. Chastened by this prospect, businesses joined ethnic groups to lobby the Judiciary Committee members to support Republican Spencer Abraham's amendment to split the legal and illegal immigration components of the bill. "Spencer Abraham got into the conservatives of the party and got a head start, and he was successful [with his amendment]," says Simpson.[59]

One example of intensive lobbying came from the Chamber of Commerce, which was worried about restrictions on the H-1B visa program to bring in temporary workers. It decided to lobby for the split-the-bill amendment because both business and ethnic groups, despite differing areas of interests in immigration policy, were "lobbying for the same thing—we were working from the same hymn book but on separate pages," according to Chamber of Commerce lobbyist Peter Eide.[60] The Chamber activated its own independent grassroots network, which includes members from local chambers, members of the national chamber, and individual companies. Once the Chamber takes an official position on a business-related legislation, it alerts its members of impending legislation and encourages them to write to their local representative and senators, toeing the Chamber's stance in these letters. Mail campaigns are very effective because these small businesses often serve as pillars of the community in most congressional districts. These small businessmen are active in local service/social organizations (such as the Elks) and are influential members of the community. Few Congressmen can afford to ignore their needs.[61]

In addition to applying behind-the-scenes pressure on individual senators, the Left-Right coalition also used an "outside" strategy to build public support mainly through the media.[62] Swartz sent media packets to over 500 editorial boards and columnists and booked numerous appearances on local television and talk-radio shows to "put a human face on the issue."[63] Prominent businessmen and columnists aided in this effort. T. J. Rodgers, the president of Cypress Semiconductors and a staunch proimmigration conservative, penned a widely discussed op-ed piece in the influential *Wall Street Journal*, praising the entrepreneurial spirit of immigrants. Swartz also worked closely with *Wall Street Journal* columnist and television talking-head Paul Gigot to dedicate proimmigration tracts in his weekly column. Think tanks provided much of the intellectual ammunition and scheduled press conferences to garner media coverage for their studies. Steven Moore of the Cato Institute, the Center for Equal Opportunity (led by Linda Chavez, a former official in the Reagan Education Department), and Empower America (headed by Jack Kemp and William Bennett) all played important roles in shaping the broader debate on immigration. Empower America, for example, produced a study called *The Leading Indicators of Immigration,* which contained generally favorable facts and figures about the contributions of immigrants to the American economy. The Alexis De Tocqueville Institute's timely study showed that immigrant workers in the high-tech area earned more than native-born workers, undermining the populist rhetoric that big business brings in "cheap" immigrant labor. These studies were widely cited in the editorial pages of numerous papers across the country.

The National Immigration Forum, the umbrella group founded by Swartz, set up lobbying-day events at Washington for both business and ethnic groups. During September 1995, over 200 people, from both liberal and conservative groups, visited congressional offices and held press conferences. The following February, over 300 representatives from ethnic and religious organizations as well as 100 business lobbyists made another round into Capitol Hill.[64] The National Immigration Forum also held numerous news conferences in major cities to publicize a report called "Together in Our Differences," which hailed immigration as good for America.

Amidst the "inside" and "outside" lobbying, the Senate Judiciary Committee supported the amendment by a 12–6 vote. Feeling the business groups' pressure, six out of the ten Republicans crossed Alan Simpson and voted for this split-the-bill amendment. The legal immigration in the Senate had died. Simpson had made a serious political error in proposing drastic changes to business immigration. His actions alarmed the business community into joining the fraying Left-Right coalition again.

After the victory in the Senate, the proimmigrationists focused their attention back to the House, this time on the floor. Representative Smith's restrictionist bill was still intact with both legal and illegal immigration provisions in it. Two freshmen Republicans, Representatives Sam Brownback and Dick Chrysler, both of whom had strong free market tendencies, offered an amendment to expunge the legal immigration component from the bill. Most of the business lobbies honored its deal with Smith not to lobby for this amendment because, as Swartz notes, "If you back out of a deal in Washington, you're dead for life."[65] Businesses, despite their previous pledge to Lamar Smith not to support a split-the-bill amendment, were eager to kill the congressman's bill. If the House bill contained a legal immigration component, Senator Simpson might reinsert harsh business provisions during the conference agreement when the differences between House and Senate bills are reconciled. Thus, behind the scenes, "Businesses were sending all sorts of signals in the House to the Republicans and the leadership that they were not taking a formal position on splitting the bill, but they told them, 'We want you [Congress] to understand that we did not oppose the splitting of the bill in the Senate, and you can draw your own conclusions,' " according to Swartz (Interview with author, April 2, 1997).

The Brownback-Chrysler Amendment hit a snag when Intel and Hewlett-Packard broke away from the coalition and started lobbying against the amendment. Apparently, some of the hi-tech companies still were not convinced of the efficacy of the split-the-bill strategy and had decided to concentrate their lobbying efforts in saving the area most dear to them: skills-based visas for businesses. In a display of Left-Right coalition dynamics at its best, Democrat Congressman Howard Berman immediately notified this development to Swartz, who called Republican Senator Abraham. His office then contacted the Hewlett-Packard and Intel lobbyists. After a lengthy meeting, Abraham convinced the two hi-tech companies to back off their opposition to the Brownback-Chrysler Amendment.

Yet this still did not ensure the passage of the amendment. The Left-Right coalition had convinced liberal legislators and the free-market conservatives to support splitting the bill. But culturally conservative Republicans had doubts about high levels of immigration. And a group of wavering Democrats was averse to killing a legal immigration package that the public as well as their president supported. The Left-Right coalition worked overtime to siphon off votes from these groups.

To sway the Democrats, Swartz convinced White House aide Rahm Emanuel to support splitting the bill. But it was the ethnic groups, most notably Asians, who played the crucial role in winning over vacillating Democrats. The Organization of Chinese Americans as early as spring of 1995 began lobbying the White House to come out against immigration reform. In a personal meeting with Vice President Al Gore, the

OCA stressed the importance of immigration to Asian-Americans, who are the fastest growing ethnic group. "Gore knows about the concerns of the Asian-American community, and he went to bat for us," says Daphne Kwok of the Organization of Chinese Americans.[66] But President Clinton had said in 1995 that the Jordan Commission's recommendations were "consistent with [his] own views." As late as February 11, 1996, he repeated his support for "lowering the level of legal immigration." Eight days later, Clinton attended an Asian-American fund-raiser that garnered a whopping $1.1 million. Then a few days later, according to the *Boston Globe*, Democratic National Committee operative John Huang—who later became embroiled in the fund-raising debacle—wrote a memo to Clinton, noting that the Asian donors' "top priority" was the opposition to the congressional immigration bill.[67] The revelation of campaign finance abuse in 1996 made it clear that the Clinton-Gore campaign received a considerable amount from wealthy Asian-American donors, and the Clinton team owed them a favor. On March 20th, Clinton reversed himself and opposed reductions in immigration, swaying a handful of Democratic votes in Congress. "The White House reversed its position 180 degrees, and we lost this crucial [Brownback-Chrysler] amendment by 20 votes. We might have defeated that amendment had the administration not reversed its position and given [the Democratic congressmen] some political cover," rues Representative Smith.[68]

While Swartz and the ethnic groups were working to win over Democrats, Grover Norquist was persuading Christian Coalition head Ralph Reed to support the amendment. In a meeting with Newt Gingrich and Reed, Norquist convinced the Christian Coalition leader to issue a letter praising the amendment as "pro-family." This letter reputedly convinced twenty to twenty-five House Republicans to vote to split the bill. When the Brownback-Chrysler amendment came up for a vote, it passed 238–183. Without these efforts by Norquist and Swartz, the House would likely have passed a bill with strong anti-legal-immigration provisions.

It should be noted that Republicans are usually less united than Democrats in their support for immigration. In fact, in most of the votes, a slim majority of Republicans voted to restrict immigration. On the Brownback-Chrysler amendment, for example, most Democrats voted for it, while only about a third of the Republicans did. The strategy usually was to convince enough libertarian-minded Republicans to join the Democrats in thwarting the restrictionists' plans. Thus, the Left-Right coalition is tilted more to the Left but it garners just enough support from the Right to defend immigration. Table 6.1 shows floor amendments for three different pieces of immigration legislation. Each amendment is labeled as either "pro-immigration" or "restrictionist." As the table reveals, Republicans—split between the libertarians and cultural conservatives—were less united than Democrats.

Although the battle was much more difficult in 1996 than in 1990, it nevertheless proved to be another victory for the Left-Right coalition. "There's a wide array of groups that think the legal immigration system is not broken and doesn't need radical changes," said Microsoft senior lawyer Ira Rubenstein in explaining the coalition politics.[69] John L. Martin, the research director of the restrictionist Center for Immigration Studies, lamented that legal immigration reform is always thwarted by "the very liberal element that is in favor of diversity in the country, business interests that benefit from a free flow of labor and people who simply don't like big government."[70]

Table 6.1
Votes on Proimmigration/Restrictionist Floor Amendments

Amendment	Yes(GOP)	No(GOP)	Yes(Dem)	No(Dem)
S. 1664 (1996) Simpson Amend: (Restriction) Reduce immigration over five years. Rejected 20-80.	13	40	7	40
HR 2202 (1996) Chrysler-Brownback Amend: (Pro-Immig) Delete legal immigration provisions. Passed 238-183.	75	158	162	25
HR 4300 (1990) Smith Amend: (Restrict) Recommit bill to committee, killing it. Rejected 176-248	137	35	39	213
Smith Amend: (Restrict) Set firmer 630,000 ceiling on immigration. Rejected 143-266.	104	56	39	210
S. 358 (1989) Hatch Amend: (Pro-Immig) Set minimum floor 216,000 for families. Passed 62-36.	25	19	37	17
HR 1510 (1984) Moorhead Amend: (Restrict) Set firmer 450,000 annual cap on immigration. Rejected 168-231.	111	46	57	185

Source: Congressional Quarterly Almanac (1984, 1989, 1990 annual editions) and various issues of *Congressional Quarterly Weekly Report.*

NEITHER LEFT NOR RIGHT: OTHER INTEREST GROUPS

Not all interest groups fit neatly into the Left-Right coalition. Some traditional opponents of immigration have moderated their views into neutrality over time. Though they may not have played a prominent role in the Left-Right coalition, these former restrictionists' neutrality was important in helping defeat restrictionist legislation. Some of these groups will be examined here.

Labor Unions

Virtually all the restrictionist laws historically have had the full support of labor unions. Unions feared that immigrants would depress wages and displace native-born workers. Racial prejudice tinged this opposition; unions have had an ugly history of anti-immigrant attitudes. In a typical testimony given by H. C. Pickering during a 1920 congressional hearing, he candidly admitted, "Our International Union of Barbers prohibits the admission of coolie or other than the white race."[71]

Yet by the 1960s, the labor unions' position had changed considerably. Polls suggest that most of the rank-and-file members still see immigrants as a competitive threat, but the official position of the leadership does not oppose family-based immigration. Several key factors explain this change. First, the merger of the American Federation of Labor with the Congress of Industrial Organizations (CIO) in 1955 tilted the union toward a more hospitable stance. The AFL had strong nativist views and did not try to recruit immigrants, while the CIO actively incorporated ethnic workers into the union.[72] As John L. Lewis, a seminal figure in the CIO, declared, "This movement stands for equality of treatment, equality of opportunity, equality of participation for every American, regardless of creed, color, nationality, or previous condition of servitude."[73] Increasing mobility and assimilation of immigrants also facilitated their incorporation into the unions. So when the two unions merged into the AFL-CIO, the union adopted the CIO's more conciliatory views.

Second, as immigration increased in the 1970s, the AFL-CIO took a long-term view. Though the influx of immigrants might temporarily put pressure on workers, these immigrants could serve as valuable foot soldiers in the labor movement in the long run. For example, the

AFL-CIO launched the Labor Immigrant and Assistance Project during the 1980s in an attempt to unionize Latino workers.[74]

Third, the AFL-CIO focused its limited resources on two forms of immigration that it saw as more serious threats: employment-based immigration and illegal immigration. The AFL-CIO feared that businesses would bring in cheap foreign workers (often temporary laborers brought under the H-1B program) to undercut American workers. It lobbied heavily for stronger regulations and a more stringent labor certification process for employment-based immigrants. "U.S. workers should have first crack at employment here, and . . . it should not be permissible for employers to use foreign workers to drive down wages or make more difficult the conditions of work," argued the AFL-CIO.[75] The AFL-CIO inveighed against illegal immigration with equal passion. As illegal immigration increased during the 1970s, the AFL-CIO began to see undocumented workers as the major threat to American labor. Illegal immigrants were often at the mercy of their employers who paid them subminimum wages in horrible working conditions; there was no way that native-born workers could compete against them. The AFL-CIO strongly supported employer sanctions to deter illegal immigration.

Finally, the AFL-CIO has moderated its views on immigration in hopes of wooing minorities as allies in its campaign for economic justice. "It's a case of rainbow politics," says Cornell labor economist Vernon Briggs, Jr., who has worked alongside labor leader Cesar Chavez. "Labor unions have been losing power and membership, so they think that they need coalitions."[76] In recent years, labor unions have actively worked with minority groups on economic issues. Last year, AFL-CIO chief John Sweeney joined Jesse Jackson and other minority leaders to support a "livable wage" bill.[77] And, in 1993, labor unions and several minority groups formed a coalition to oppose the North American Free Trade Agreement. Other issues on which they have worked together in the past decade include minimum wage, anti-right-to-work laws, and D.C. statehood.

Though the AFL-CIO cannot be described as a strong supporter of immigration, it cannot be classified as a strict restrictionist, either. It is generally accepting of family-based immigration, but it has strong reservations against employment-based visas and illegal immigration. Yet this change—from a staunch restrictionist in the early twentieth century to the current position of accommodation—has greatly strengthened the hand of the proimmigration bloc because it no longer has to face such a politically formidable opponent.

Local and State Governments

During the nineteenth century era of open borders, individual states and local governments receiving a large percentage of immigrants lobbied the federal government to erect barriers. Though states at the time had a very limited welfare safety net, they nevertheless argued that immigrants were a burden on the government as well as on private charities. Fiscal cost, however, was not the major reason for restrictionism. Their aversion toward immigration was rooted in racial prejudice and concern for public order.

Like most of their peers of the time, local and state government officials had unenlightened racial views. States that received a huge influx of immigrants felt that they were being invaded by foreigners. "And when we find this occupation by a foreign people, unassimilable with the white races, coming here to destroy, it is a mere assertion of the fundamental right of self-preservation that fixes the policy," said California Senator James D. Phelan in urging the federal government to halt immigration.[78] And since most of these immigrants were disenfranchised, local and state leaders could pillory them with minimal adverse political consequences.

Prodded by demagogic racial appeals by the likes of Senator Phelan, violence against immigrants became a major problem for local and state governments. One congressional witness explained the violence and public mayhem caused by anti-immigrant fever: "I saw school children when school was out pick up brickbats and stones and stone the Chinese and beat their faces into pulp. . . . We burned to death two score of Chinese in their shacks—a mob did—and when the poor wretches rushed out to escape the fire they were shot and clubbed to death. They were robbed, murdered, maltreated, as you know, all over California."[79] Other ethnic groups were targeted as well. For example, violent riots directed toward Italian workers spread throughout the country. Local and state government officials, even if they did not hold racist views, wanted to limit immigration in order to maintain public order. A Washington congressman, worried by the outbreaks of violence, explained, "A law should be enacted restricting Japanese immigration to this coast, not only for the good of our own people, but for the good of the Japanese."[80] Consequently, state and local governments lobbied the federal government for restrictionist laws. As one California judge testified, "The States cannot do it. It is a national question."[81]

By the 1970s, local and state governments no longer lobbied against immigration and, instead, only demanded reimbursement from the federal government for social services. This was made possible by the increase in federal largesse and the decline of racism among both policymakers and the public. It is telling that California, which once spawned inveterate racists like Senator Phelan, had elected S. I. Hayakawa, a Japanese American, to the United States Senate in 1976. And as the number of immigrants who could vote increased in urban areas, local and state government officials found it politically suicidal to use racial appeals or to call for limitations on immigration. In fact, many of today's local and state government officials, such as New York City mayor Rudolph Giuliani and New York governor George Pataki are decisively proimmigrant.

Also, violence against immigrants abated markedly as the public became less xenophobic. There were still isolated incidents of violence, but it was no longer an issue of public order. The main issue over immigration was now about federal reimbursement for social welfare programs that had burgeoned since the 1960s. "It should be recognized that Federal immigration policies, in effect, have mandated enormous costs on communities in which aliens resettle," testified Mark A. Tajima, a legislative analyst at the County of Los Angeles. "Because it is the national interest which is served by immigration policies and it is the Federal government which determines those policies, the Federal government should also bear the financial responsibility for their costs."[82] Local and state governments—which have large ethnic groups as part of their constituency—found it politically advantageous to demand the federal government to defray the fiscal costs of accommodating the immigrants. This strategy allows local and state governments to appease the critics of immigration who complain about its fiscal costs, yet not offend the foreign-born population. The local and state governments' neutrality on immigration levels meant that restrictionists had lost yet another powerful ally, making it that much more difficult to achieve their goal.

African-American Groups

During a WBAI-FM New York radio show in 1990, a black woman named Hazel Dukes bluntly said what many African Americans furtively feel about immigration. "Why let foreigners, newcomers, have these jobs while blacks, who have been here for hundreds of years, can't support themselves or their families?" she asked.[83] Hazel Dukes, however, is not any ordinary black woman: she is a prominent civil rights leader and the president of the New York chapter of the National Association for the Advancement of Colored People (NAACP). The black civil rights establishment—which is staunchly proimmigration—quickly rebuked her. A chastened Dukes apologized, and, in an amazing display of verbal gymnastics, she "clarified" her statement into an indictment on the work ethic of blacks. "I was saying that if foreigners can come into this country and work in hotels in jobs once held by us, then African-Americans can to[o]. Go get a job; that's what I was saying," she later feebly explained.[84]

Duke's initial brusqueness aside, she had a point: high levels of immigration—although probably beneficial to the American economy on the whole—can have an adverse impact on low-skilled workers, who are disproportionately black. "Competition from immigrants, while not the only factor to explain the low labor-force participant rates of black males, must be included with any such list of negative influences," notes Vernon Briggs, Jr., a Cornell University labor economist who has written several books on immigration.[85] Although empirical data remain nebulous, anecdotal evidence supports the view that blacks employed in well-paying jobs like janitorial work in Los Angeles in the 1970s were replaced by Mexican immigrants willing to work for lower wages. In large urban areas where most immigrants end up settling, it is rare to see black busboys or hotel cleaning ladies anymore.

Not surprisingly, blacks oppose immigration at higher rates than any other racial group. Yet black civil rights groups such as the NAACP and the National Urban League do not reflect the opinion held by most rank-and-file African Americans. "We don't support the thesis that immigration hurts African Americans," says Robert McAlpine, the Washington director of public policy and government relations of the National Urban League.[86] Added one former director of the NAACP Washington Bureau: "Immigration is now and always has been good for America."

On issues like affirmative action and welfare, black civil rights groups play an active role in Washington, always quick to defend the interests of African Americans. But this is not so when it comes to immigration. When Congress voted to increase legal immigration by a whopping 40% in 1990, African-American groups were absolutely indifferent, ignoring the negative impact that such a mass increase might have on the black community. And when the 104th Congress considered reducing legal immigration by a third, no African-American organization bothered testifying at the hearings. Frank Morris, a dean at the historically black Morgan State University, was the only African American to speak in favor of the bill. "Not all Americans have benefited from an immigrant experience especially in times of large scale mass immigration," he told Congress.[87] "Too often the true impact of our current immigration policies on African-American communities is either ignored, distorted, or not considered important enough to be given great weight."[88] Morris's recommendations, however, were largely ignored by most congressmen, who are more solicitous to powerful political interest groups than to academics. Had political heavyweights like the NAACP lobbied in favor of the bill, it might have fared better in Congress.

Why don't civil rights groups oppose high levels of immigration, especially when this seems to be against the interest of so many inner-city blacks? Undoubtedly, some of it is attributable to the affinity that they feel toward people of color fleeing oppression. Yet there is also a self-serving political rationale behind it. Out of the around 800,000 annual immigrants, nearly 80% come from Third World nations. As birth rates of native-born Americans steadily decline, immigration is becoming a large source of population growth in the United States. If current demographic trends continue, whites will likely become a numerical minority by the year 2050, according to the Census Bureau.

This "browning" of America is appealing to civil rights groups because it means a dilution of whites' power, a turning of the table of sorts. It also means a larger constituency and hence increased political clout for civil rights leaders. Lost amidst all the recent talk about the gender gap and soccer moms is the clout of minority voters in presidential elections. Whites have voted increasingly Republican in the past several elections, while around 80% of blacks and Hispanics have voted Democratic. In 1992 and 1996, both George Bush and Bob Dole, despite their decisive losses to Bill Clinton, received a plurality of the white vote. To put it in other words, Clinton would have lost both elections had minorities not overwhelmingly voted Democratic. Civil rights groups are quite aware of this fact. As whites become increasingly fiscally conservative and hostile to race-based policies, the minority vote may be the only thing that can save an activist government.

"We [blacks and Hispanics] have common interests on many issues," explains Sylvia Brooks, the president of the National Urban League of Houston, a city with a high Hispanic immigrant population. "Education is a big issue in Texas because the state university is trying to reduce the number of minority students. Without affirmative action, many minority black and Hispanic students would not be in school. And welfare reform will affect both immigrants and African Americans."[89]

But Brooks sees the "browning" of America as the saving grace. "Hispanics will probably be the majority population by around the year 2007 in Houston. And in many places, we [blacks and Hispanics] already are the majority population," she gleefully notes. "We need to be active and get our fair representation, so we can retain the opportunities we've earned and get the changes that we want."[90]

Brooks isn't the only one who feels this way. Following Jesse Jackson's vision of a Rainbow Coalition, Ben Chavis made waves a couple of years ago as the president of the NAACP when he announced a concerted effort to forge a coalition among all people of color. "The demographics of America have changed. . . . There's a browning of America," he said. "That's why I don't want to change the name. The National Association for the Advancement of Colored People—people of color—is right on target. We want the NAACP to be a leading instrument to transform our society into a more multiracial, multicultural, multilingual society that values diversity instead of fearing it." He added, "The NAACP does not see a conflict between African-Americans and immigrants."[91]

Black leaders are especially eager to court Latinos, the fastest-growing ethnic group in America. "We basically try to be supportive of the policies of groups like the National Council of La Raza and the Mexican-American Legal Defense Fund. We're concerned and sensitive to their concerns," says McAlpine of the National Urban League.[92] The power of the Latino vote was evident in the 1996 presidential election. Latinos voted overwhelmingly for Democrats, allowing them to win bedrock GOP states like Arizona and Florida, which had not voted Democratic since 1948 and 1976, respectively. And Republican Congressman Bob Dornan was ousted by an unimpressive political neophyte Loretta Sanchez, thanks in part to the mobilization of Latino voters in the working-class California congressional district.[93]

Not all black leaders support high levels of immigration. The late Congresswoman Barbara Jordan, who headed the prestigious United States Commission on Immigration Reform, recommended curtailing immigration levels by a third. But on the whole, the black leadership in America has been a dependable supporter of immigration. What this means for restrictionists is that they have lost out on a potentially powerful ally.

CONCLUSION

Since 1965, immigration to the United States has increased dramatically, and attempts to curtail it have been thwarted every time. This success is in stark contrast to what occurred in the period between 1921 and 1964 when Congress repeatedly placed draconian restrictions on immigration. The post-1965 era of liberal immigration policy can be attributed to an unusual but powerful Left-Right interest group coalition. The coalescing of conservatives and liberals was facilitated by two major developments in recent decades: the civil rights movement and the ascendancy of conservative economics in a globalized economy, which empowered ethnic groups and strengthened Republican support for immigration, respectively. Furthermore, the refusal of labor unions and state governments to lobby against immigration strengthened the political clout of proimmigration forces.

Yet the public opinion is still hostile to this expansionist legislation. The next chapter will discuss how policymakers shield themselves from a potential public backlash. One way is to focus on the valence issue of 'family values' when discussing immigration. The other method is to channel the public discontent onto the problem of illegal immigration.

NOTES

1. Holly Idelson, "House Panel Opens Debate on Major Restrictions," *Congressional Quarterly Weekly Report*, 23 September 1995, p. 2912.

2. Ibid., p. 2912.

3. Several scholars have pointed out this Left-Right alliance. For example, see Peter H. Schuck, "The Politics of Rapid Legal Change: Immigration Policy in the 1980s," Marc K. Landy and Martin A. Levin, eds., *The New Politics of Public Policy* (Baltimore: The Johns Hopkins University Press, 1995), pp. 47–87, and Daniel J. Tichenor, "The Politics of Immigration Reform in the United States, 1981–1990," *Polity* 26 (1984): 333–63.

4. Yale law professor Peter H. Schuck hypothesizes that ideas drove immigration reform in the 1980s. He attributes ideas for building coalitions, changing beliefs, mobilizing symbols, reinforcing existing regimes, and re-

ducing dissonance. See Schuck, "The Politics of Rapid Legal Change: Immigration Policy in the 1980s," pp. 47–87.

5. Interviewed by author, April 11, 1997.

6. Interviewed by author, April 11, 1997.

7. Patrick J. McDonnell, "Immigrants a Net Economic Plus, Study Says," *Los Angeles Times*, 18 May 1997, p. A3.

8. Robert Bartley, *The Seven Fat Years* (New York: Free Press, 1992), p. 26.

9. Ibid., p. 27.

10. George Gilder, *Wealth and Poverty* (New York: Basic Books, 1981), p. 67.

11. George Gilder, *Spirit of Enterprise* (New York: Simon & Schuster, 1984), p. 54.

12. George Will, "Liberals, Racism and Asian-Americans," *St. Louis Post-Dispatch*, 18 April 1989, p. 3B.

13. David Brand, "The New Whiz Kids: Why Asian Americans Are Doing So Well, and What It Costs Them," *Time*, 31 August 1987, p. 42.

14. Kenneth Lee, "Let's Sell More U.S. Visas," *American Enterprise*, March/April 1997, p. 76.

15. U.S. Congress, House Subcommittee on Immigration and Claims, *Immigration in the National Interest Act of 1995: Hearings*, 104th Congress, 1st Session, 1995, p. 106.

16. Tom Mashberg, "Crossing the Boundaries—Politicians Haggle on the Future of Immigration," *Boston Herald*, 20 October 1996, p. 5.

17. Marc Sandalow, "GOP Divided over Immigration," *San Francisco Chronicle*, 27 February 1996, p. A2.

18. U.S. Congress, House Subcommittee on Immigration, Refugees and International Law, and Immigration Task Force of the Committee on Education and Labor, *Immigration Act of 1989 (Part 3): Hearings*, 101st Congress, 2d Session, 1989, p. 269.

19. Ibid., p. 918.

20. House Subcommittee, *Immigration in the National Interest Act of 1995*, p. 193.

21. U.S. Congress, House Committee on Immigration and Naturalization, *Japanese Immigration: Hearings*, 66th Congress, 2nd Session, 1921, p. 25.

22. U.S. Congress, House Committee on Immigration and Naturalization. *Biological Aspects of Immigration: Hearings*, 66th Congress, 2d Session, 1921, p. 3.

23. U.S. Congress, Senate Committee on the Judiciary, *The Immigration and Naturalization Systems of the United States: Report of the Committee on the Judiciary Pursuant to S. Res. 137*, 80th Congress, 1st session, 1950, p. 455.

24. David M. Reimers, *Still the Golden Door: The Third World Comes to America* (New York: Columbia University Press), p. 67.

25. Ibid., p. 82.

26. Nadine Cohodas, "Senate Passes Immigration Reform Bill," *Congressional Quarterly Weekly Report*, 21 May 1983, p. 1006.

27. U.S. Congress, House Committee on the Judiciary, *Family Unity and Employment Opportunity Immigration Act of 1990*, 101st Congress, 2d Session, 1990, H. Rept. 101–723, p. 48.

28. FAIR, however, suffers from the "collective action" problem as described by political scientist Mancur Olson. Because it deals with a public good, FAIR has problems attracting members and lacks the clout or resources of, say, businesses. In the past, groups dedicated solely to restricting immigration may have had more success in recruiting members—despite the lack of divisible goods—by appealing to a base emotion like racism. But, today, groups like FAIR cannot appeal to such powerful emotion and, instead, rely on a hodgepodge of issues like population growth that do not have the same resonance as racial appeals. As former Senator Alan Simpson pointed out, "FAIR is a thoughtful group, but they just don't have the same clout or the power of the people who raise the Statue of Liberty." Interview by author with Alan Simpson, April 11, 1997.

29. Interviewed by author, April 11, 1997.

30. Rob Gurwitt and Nadine Cohodas, "Hispanic-Asian Boycott: a Gesture Fizzles," *Congressional Quarterly Weekly Report*, 21 July 1984, p. 1733.

31. U.S. Immigration and Naturalization Service, *Statistical Yearbook of the Immigration and Naturalization Service, 1994* (Washington, D.C.: U.S. Government Printing Office, 1996), p. 160.

32. Schuck, p. 69.

33. U.S. Congress, House Subcommittee on Immigration, Refugees and International Law, *Immigration Act of 1989 (Part 1): Hearings*, 101st Congress, 1st Session, 1989, p. 244.

34. Interviewed by author, March 31, 1997.

35. Gilder gave Swartz $50,000 in 1990. Howard Berkowitz and John Holman, two other benefactors, each contributed $25,000 to Swartz for his coalition-building efforts. Personal correspondence from Swartz to Dick Gilder, Howard Berkowitz, and John Holman, July 4, 1995, papers from the Office of Rick Swartz & Associates.

36. Plan of Action memo and memorandum from Rick Swartz to Dick Gilder, March 6, 1990, papers from the Office of Rick Swartz & Associates.

37. Memorandum from the papers from the Office of Rick Swartz & Associates.

38. House Subcommittee, *Immigration Act of 1989 (Part 1)*, p. 437.

39. Memorandum, June 23, 1990, papers from the Office of Rick Swartz & Associates.

40. House Subcommittee, *Immigration Act of 1989 (Part 3)*, p. 3.

41. Interviewed by author, April 2, 1997.

42. Interviewed by author, April 2, 1997.

43. Interviewed by author, March 31, 1997.

44. House Subcommittee, *Immigration Act of 1989 (Part 1)*, p. 270.

45. Daniel J. Tichenor, "The Politics of Immigration Reform in the United States, 1981–1990," *Polity* 26 (1984): 352.

46. For example, Representative Lamar Smith offered a floor amendment to recommit the bill to committee, thereby killing it. The amendment was rejected 176–248 with the key help of several dozen Republicans who strayed from most of their other GOP colleagues.

47. Memorandum, October 4, 1990, papers from the Office of Rick Swartz & Associates.

48. Personal correspondence from Rick Swartz, July 4, 1995, papers from the Office of Rick Swartz & Associates. Among the prominent members of the Left-Right coalition in 1996 were the Cato Institute, the Center for Equal Opportunity, Empower America, the Committee for Small Business Survival, the National Federation of Independent Businesses, the National Association of Manufacturers, Citizens for a Sound Economy, the Chamber of Commerce, Americans for Tax Reforms, the U.S. Catholic Conference, the American Jewish Committee, the National Council of La Raza, the American Bar Association, the Organization of Chinese Americans, and various individual businesses.

49. Interviewed by author, March 31, 1997.

50. Interviewed by author, April 2, 1997.

51. Interviewed by author, March 31, 1997.

52. John Heilemann, "Do you know the way to Ban Jose?" *Wired*, August 1996, p. 176.

53. Interviewed by author, March 31, 1997.

54. David Masci, "Panel OKs Restrictions on Legal Immigrants," *Congressional Quarterly Weekly Report*, 2 December 1995, p. 3656.

55. Ibid., p. 3656.

56. Heilemann, "Ban Jose," p. 176.

57. Interviewed by author, March 31, 1997.

58. Interviewed by author, April 11, 1997.

59. Interviewed by author, April 11, 1997.

60. Interviewed by author, April 4, 1997.

61. See the case studies in Norman J. Ornstein and Shirley Elder, *Interest Groups, Lobbying and Policymaking* (Washington, D.C.: Congressional Quarterly Press, 1978).

62. For an explanation of inside and outside lobbying, see Dennis S. Ippolito and Thomas G. Walker, *Political Parties, Interest Groups, and Public Policy: Group Influence in American Politics* (Englewood Cliffs, N.J.: Prentice Hall, 1980).

63. Strategy memo, August 27, 1995, papers from the Office of Rick Swartz & Associates.

64. Memorandum, February 29, 1996, papers from the Office of Rick Swartz & Associates.

65. Interviewed by author, March 31, 1997.

66. Interviewed by author, April 2, 1997.

67. Michael Kranish, "Clinton Policy Shift Followed Asian-American Fund-Raiser," *Boston Globe*, 15 January 1997, p. A1.

68. Interviewed by author, March 31, 1997.

69. Matthew Purdy, "Unlikely Allies Battle Congress over Anti-Immigration Plans," *New York Times*, 11 October 1995, p. B1.

70. Ibid., p. B1.

71. House Committee, *Japanese Immigration*, p. 1389.

72. Thomas Gobel, "Becoming American: Ethnic Workers and the Rise of the CIO," George E. Pozzetta, ed., *Unions and Immigrants: Organization and Struggle* (New York: Garland Publishing, 1991), pp. 61–94.

73. As quoted in ibid., p. 92.

74. Robert Lazo, "Latinos and the AFL-CIO: The California Immigrant Workers Association as an Important New Development," Antoinette Sedillo Lopez, ed., *Latino Employment, Labor Organizations and Immigration* (New York: Garland Publishing, 1995), p. 37.

75. House Subcommittee, *Immigration in the National Interest Act of 1995*, p. 341.

76. Interviewed by author, March 31, 1997.

77. Jim Kirk, "AFL-CIO Chief Backs Jobs Bill; Details Union Plans to Rainbow Coalition," *Chicago Sun-Times*, 2 March 1996, p. 28.

78. House Committee, *Japanese Immigration*, p. 4.

79. Ibid., p. 43.

80. Ibid., p. 1291.

81. Ibid., p. 483.

82. House Subcommittee, *Immigration Act of 1989 (Part 3)*, p. 610.

83. David Gonzalez, "Criticism Aimed at Statements on Immigrants," *New York Times*, 5 October 1990, p. B3.

84. T. J. Collins and Molly Gurdy, "Immigrants Vow Lawsuit against NAACP's Dukes," *New York Newsday*, 13 October 1990, p. 4.

85. Interviewed by author, March 31, 1997.

86. Interviewed by author, February 1997.

87. House Subcommittee, *Immigration in the National Interest Act of 1995*, p. 155.

88. Ibid., p. 155.

89. Interviewed by author, February 1997.

90. Interviewed by author, February 1997.

91. Melita Marie Garza, "NAACP Director Aims to Join Blacks and Browns," *Chicago Tribune*, 11 July 1994, p. 1.

92. Interviewed by author, February 1997.

93. Kenneth Lee, "Hasta La Vista," *New Republic*, 27 October 1997, p. 13.

Chapter 7

Insulation from Public Opinion: The Politics of Family and Illegal Immigration

Janaki Manian, a Detroit-based psychiatrist who immigrated from India, has been trying to bring her older brother to America for ten years. Her brother has yet to receive a visa because of the interminable backlogs for countries like India, where thousands of people patiently wait for years to receive a vaunted visa to the United States. This waiting game is a rite-of-passage for would-be Americans, who have little choice but to wait to hear from the American embassy. Janaki's hopes of her brother coming to the United States were nearly dashed in 1996 when Congress considered a bill that would have completely eliminated the preference category for adult brothers and sisters, one of the most common ways that immigrants come to the United States in our current system of family preferences. Without this family connection, it is nearly impossible for anyone to come to the United States, unless he or she possesses extraordinary skills or talents. "It's really disappointing they want to wipe it out completely," Manian told the *New York Times* at the time. "Having gone through all this paperwork and phone calls, I think it's fair to let people in who applied 10 or 15 years ago."[1] Fortunately for Manian, the legal immigration reform provisions in the congressional bills were stricken and never enacted. And her brother still had a spot in the long waiting list to receive that ticket to America.

This is the type of heart-rending story that immigration enthusiasts shrewdly cite to restructure the terms of the debate in their favor.

Political rhetoric—how an issue is framed and structured—is important in the formulation of public policy because it can help shift the public opinion toward one side over the other. Take the issue of affirmative action. If affirmative action is framed in terms of preferential treatment, most Americans strongly oppose it, viewing it as anathema to American ideals. But if it is asked in terms of affording more opportunities to racial minorities, more Americans support it. Hence, opponents of affirmative action denounce it as reverse racism, while supporters argue that it only levels the playing field for minorities. In reality, both statements are true: affirmative action involves both affording more opportunities to minorities *and* discriminating against whites. Each side, however, will only use the most advantageous political rhetoric to shore up public support.[2] Similarly, one way proimmigration activists have built public support for their cause has been to frame immigration through the political rhetoric of the family. Another reason why political rhetoric is important is that it can "stitch together seemingly separate interests and thereby allow collective action to occur."[3] The family can bind diverse groups—conservatives or liberals, Republicans or Democrats, blacks or whites—because very few people will publicly impugn the family.

Unfortunately for the restrictionist camp, it has ended up on the short end of the stick in the battle over political rhetoric. But that was not always the case. In previous decades, restrictionists had successfully framed the debate in their favor. In short, the political rhetoric of the family is a relatively new development.

IN THE NAME OF THE FAMILY

For most of the nineteenth century and well into the twentieth century, restrictionists had depended heavily on racialistic and ethnocentric rhetoric to limit the number of Catholics, Chinese, Slavs, and other "undesirables." This view had the support of both policymakers and the public. Indeed, the ethnocentric national origins quota system served as the cornerstone of America's immigration policy for a large part of the twentieth century. Such arguments, however, were no longer socially acceptable by the mid-1960s as the civil rights ethos had liberalized the racial views of most Americans. As nationalist organizations like the Immigration Restrictionist League faded away, so did overtly ethnocentric arguments against immigration.

Another common argument historically adduced by restrictionists was an economic one: many Americans feared that immigrants would depress wages or displace native-born workers. This perception was based mostly on coarse anecdotes; very few studies in the early twentieth century actually measured the impact of immigration on the labor force. A typical testimony was given by the secretary of the barbers' union during a 1920 congressional hearing: "I know that it [immigration] affects the labor situation, because everybody who works in the catering industry has to compete with the Jap. . . . The Japanese by their low standard of living can work so much cheaper, and they work much longer hours in the restaurants."[4] No statistics or studies were cited in most of the testimonies. Not one academic or economist testified during these hearings. In fact, a large number of the witnesses were average private citizens who had little expertise in any area but felt compelled to expound their personal views on immigration.

The rise of professionalism and the "expert" class in recent decades, however, has demanded more accurate and rigorous empirical data. Today, no matter what the issue, there needs to be voluminous studies and "expert" testimonies. Rarely do we see ordinary private citizens being invited to congressional testimonies to detail their own personal opinions. The growth in the importance of university research and think tanks in the past half-century reflects this increasing dependence on "scientific" studies for policy-making. In the area of immigration, academics from places such as Cornell University and University of Maryland, as well as researchers from think tanks like the American Enterprise Institute routinely have testified in front of Congress in recent years.

But unlike, say, welfare programs—whose fiscal costs can be easily measured as a part of the federal budget—the economic costs of immigration, as determined by its impact on wages and labor participation, are nebulous. It is very difficult to ascertain whether an immigrant displaces a native worker or if he takes a job that a native-born American is unwilling to work at. Economists constantly spar in both the academic and popular press over whether immigration is a boon or a bane. University of Maryland economist Julian Simon, for example, argues that immigration is an unmitigated good for the country, while others like Harvard economist George Borjas and Cornell University professor Vernon Briggs, Jr., hold a more jaundiced view.[5] At one point during the 1990 congressional hearings, a frustrated Representative Lamar Smith asked one of the witnesses, "There is some dramatically conflicting testimony that we have gotten today. You are on one side; someone else is on the other side. Who is to say who is correct?"[6]

The inconclusive nature of economic data was most evident during the joint congressional hearings of the immigration subcommittee and the Labor and Education Committee, which convened specifically to examine the impact of immigration on the labor market. Witnesses from the Labor Department could not give an accurate assessment of immigration's effect on the labor market. "I would like to point out at this time, however, that we currently have no data systems that would allow us to make judgments" necessary to determine employer need for immigrants, testified David O. Williams, the deputy assistant labor secretary.[7] This theme of technical inadequacy was repeated throughout the hearings. "Even if we were to find that some of the required variables could be measured with acceptable reliability, meeting the needs of those who implement immigration policy would still require the making of judgments that fall outside the area of expertise of a statistical agency," said Janet L. Norwood, the commissioner of the Bureau of Labor Statistics.[8] When congressmen queried Labor Department officials on specific areas, they received similar responses:

> *Rep. Morrison:* Would you say that is a common condition in our labor force of these training gaps being gaps that have a very long lead time to be filled?
>
> *Ms. Norwood:* I believe from the data that I see that it is really very difficult to determine—for example, take the case of nurses—whether the problem is that there is just a shortage of nurses or whether the conditions under which nurses are working are not adequate to encourage people to go into that . . . we know very little about the supply of labor, the people who are not in the labor force. We don't even know what training they have. . . . There is very little known about the type of training, the caliber of training, how up to date training is, even of people in the labor force, let alone those out of the labor force. We don't know very much about what kinds of conditions or wage levels would be required to get people who are not now working to come in and ask for a job.[9]

This frustrating exchange of questions and "non-answers" was pervasive throughout the testimonies. In short, the economic case against immigrants has less cogency today than it did seventy or eighty years ago because there is little empirical data to prove conclusively that immigrants hurt Americans. Such data was lacking during the restrictionist era as well, but there was less emphasis on "scientific" studies and "expert" testimonies back then, and anecdotal evidence was often deemed sufficient.

With both the race and economic issues not as salient (though still important) in the political rhetoric of immigration as they were earlier in the century, the focus turned to the family. The Immigration Act of 1965, by making family reunification the cornerstone of immigration policy, made family the main currency in the political rhetoric of immigration. Like other countries, America has always considered the family to be paramount, but it became virtually sacrosanct by the end of the 1960s. In yet another fortuitous circumstance for proimmigrationists, the family began to fray starting in the sixties. Out-of-wedlock births skyrocketed among all races, with about two-thirds of black babies being born by single mothers. The rate of illegitimacy among inner-city blacks reached the astounding rate of nearly 90%. Teenage pregnancies exploded as well. Media reports of twelve or thirteen year-olds giving birth became so common that they were no longer deemed "newsworthy." And divorce, once unspeakable, became a fact-of-life, with one out of every two marriages ending in failure.

Many Americans were alarmed and horrified by these trends. A backlash emerged against the sexual revolution, which was no longer seen as liberating but, rather, as destructive. As Lisa Schriffen, a speechwriter for Dan Quayle, recalled her childhood in Greenwich Village: "New York City then [in the 1960s] was a very libertine place, and everyone I knew was divorced. I soon realized that the sexual revolution led to misery rather than fulfillment, that divorce did not leave families better off and happier."[10] Best-selling books with titles such as *A Divorce Culture, The Abolition of Marriage,* and *The Assault on Parenthood* chronicled the destruction of the two-parent family. Vice President Dan Quayle even devoted an entire speech in 1992 to lambaste Murphy Brown for giving birth out-of-wedlock. Although he was initially ridiculed for chiding a fictional television character, his point that the family was in crisis resonated among many Americans, not just conservative partisans. Only a year after Quayle's speech, sociologist Barbara Dafoe Whitehead wrote an essay, "Dan Quayle was Right," in the *Atlantic Monthly,* hardly a redoubt of right-wing thought.[11]

Whatever the cause for this decline, most Americans agreed that the family had to be strengthened. If we failed to strengthen it, mass social chaos would result. Thus, the family became an important valence issue; no one wanted to appear antifamily. The idea of "family values" has become a mainstay of our political parlance. Even Hillary Clinton, often depicted as a radical feminist by conservatives, felt compelled to say that she is ambivalent about no-fault divorce when children are involved.[12] To appear to be against "family values" is to oppose mom and apple pie. Just as important, the family was something that could bind disparate political groups. Politicians as diverse as Bill Clinton, Ralph Reed, and Donna Shalala could all agree on the primacy of the family. And in politics, coalition is paramount.

Proimmigration groups intentionally seized this valence issue to their benefit. According to immigration lobbyist Rick Swartz, "Of course, there was an intentional focus on the family. When you see the polling data, Americans generally think there is too much immigration and [immigrants] are causing so many problems. But when you put a human face [on it] and ask should an immigrant be allowed to bring his wife to the U.S., then they think about a real-life family and you get a more sympathetic reaction from the public, and the same thing works for Congress."[13] Thus, any attempts to curtail immigration were quickly denounced as anti-family. Many of the restrictionists tried to counter the antifamily charges by portraying their attempts to reduce immigration as the true profamily view, but they ended up sounding defensive.

The Family and Immigration Debate, 1996

Representative Lamar Smith's and Senator Alan Simpson's restrictionist bills alarmed the proimmigrationists into action, and political rhetoric played an important role in structuring the debate. Proimmigration legislators excoriated the bill as antifamily because it abolished the preference category for siblings and adult children and set a firmer cap on family-based immigration. "In a Congress which heralds family values as its prevailing theme, this bill is extreme antifamily legislation. Restrictions to family reunification in this bill ensure that American families may be forever separated from their loved ones. . . . [The bill] hurts families, it hurts children," said Nancy Pelosi (D-Calif.).[14] Representative Robert Menendez (D-N.J.), in a speech on the floor of Congress, argued that opposition to family reunification contravened American values and tradition:

> The cuts in legal immigration hurt family reunification efforts and show the hypocrisy of a Congress that promotes family values. Why does this "family friendly" Congress want to prohibit the adult sons, daughters,

brothers and sisters of U.S. citizens from entering the country? Legal immigration reinforces family structure, upholds family values, and benefits the nation. Creating a hardship for U.S. citizens by permanently separating them from their close family members does not promote family values. It disintegrates the fabric of American values and jeopardizes the Nation's future.[15]

Other representatives accused supporters of the bill of being accomplices in the decline of the family. "The current legal immigration system is specifically designed to strengthen families by reuniting close family members. . . . We must not abandon these principles. At a time when strong family bonds are more important than ever, restrictions in family based immigration will hurt legal immigrant families in America," claimed Representative Sheila Jackson-Lee.[16]

It wasn't just the Democrats who used the family rhetoric. Republicans like Senator Mike DeWine of Ohio denounced the bills as antifamily, showing the power of political rhetoric to create unlikely coalitions. He lamented that the bill "undermines the family structure. And, frankly, in the history of civilization there has never been a stronger support structure than the family. . . . We talk in this Congress a lot about family values. We talk about how important families are. They are important. . . . [The bill] is antifamily. It is antifamily reunification and goes against the tradition of trying to attract the best people in this country."[17] When Simpson offered an amendment on the floor of the Senate to reinsert his expunged legal immigration provisions, DeWine countered, "I believe that the Simpson amendment is in fact antifamily, antifamily reunification, and goes against the best traditions of this country. . . . That is antifamily. It is wrong. It is wrong. We should not do it."[18]

Proimmigration legislators were taking their cue from interest groups. Religious organizations used the family political rhetoric to defend family-reunification immigration. "The family unit is the basic building block of any society. In the United States, the family is under siege at all levels. . . . Yet, part of the disintegration of the nuclear family itself lies in the loosening of bonds between wider family units. Where extended families have previously provided a cushion enabling nuclear families to weather difficult times, those supports have often been eroded," explained John Swenson of the United States Catholic Conference. "It is important that, as a nation, we recognize the importance of affirming family within the immigration context as a means of not only affirming the family in the U.S. in general, but as a means of providing buffers for immigrants who seek to acclimate to this society."[19]

Ethnic lobbyists, who have considerable influence over Democrats and congressmen representing heavily ethnic districts, put special emphasis on the family. They stressed the primacy of family members—even extended family members—in the Asian and Latin cultures. "Families are the backbone of our nation. Family unit promotes the stability, health and productivity of family members and contributes to the economic and social welfare of the United States," testified Karen Narasaki, the executive director of the National Asian Pacific American Legal Consortium.[20] Raul Yzaguirre of the National Council of La Raza tried to downplay the abstract numerical level of immigration and, instead, emphasized the emotional value of family. "The policy debate, similarly, should focus more attention on the types of immigrants who are admitted than on abstract numerical levels. If the debate simply focuses on a number and possible additions or subtractions to it, it will lose sight of the important fact that any reduction in levels could mean that American families or businesses will have to wait in longer lines to reunite with their closest family members or to bring in a needed employee."[21] Later, ethnic groups admitted that this family rhetoric was intentionally designed to woo support from groups not traditionally known for their support of immigration. "In 1996 in particular, we used family rhetoric—the whole concept of family—because of the Christian Coalition, and the right-wing thing, and their emphasis on the family. That was one way they were brought into this whole debate," said Daphne Kwok of the Organization of Chinese Americans.[22]

The relevance of this "profamily" political rhetoric is that it struck at the Achilles' heel of the restrictionists' argument. Virtually all public opinion polls show that most Americans want to decrease immigration, and they agree with the restrictionists that immigrants burden the social welfare system, displace American workers, and balkanize the country. Yet, as the chapter on public opinion polls showed, most Americans are lenient when it comes to family reunification. Because the family enjoys a sacrosanct position in the hearts of Americans, most people want families of all ethnicities to be reunited. Indeed, people are more likely to support visas for family reunification than for business/economic reasons or for refugees. In other words, immigration supporters turned the debate upside-down by putting the restrictionists on the defensive. As Raul Yzaguirre of the National Council of La Raza reminded Congress, "When the kinds of people who immigrate to the United

States are described, public opinion is much more likely to be supportive."[23] This doesn't mean that the proimmigration congressmen were completely insulated from public opinion; rather, the framing of the issue in terms of the family mitigated the opposition among the public, and legislators felt safer in supporting immigration. It should also be noted that proimmigrationists were not necessarily being candid in their encomium to the family—many of them were using it only as a political strategy—but it was effective in turning the tables of public opinion. In particular, the political rhetoric stung Republicans, many of whom may have had some restrictionist leanings, but also prided themselves in being profamily. In a mighty blow to restrictionist Republicans, the Christian Coalition came out in support for the Chrysler-Brownback amendment which expunged the legal immigration restrictions from the bill, and lauded the amendment as profamily. That statement is credited with swaying twenty to twenty-five Republican votes.

Restrictionists were clearly flustered by how the issue was being framed by the political rhetoric of family. Representative Lamar Smith lamented that, "It is an easy issue to demagogue, and it lends itself to emotionalism. I stressed [during floor and committee debate] that we need to resist emotion and embrace reason when it comes to immigration."[24] Senator Richard Shelby (R-Ala.) bluntly tried to counter the charges of being antifamily head-on:

> They [proimmigrationists] imply that we do not support family values if we do not support allowing every immigrant who comes here to later bring his or her entire extended family. Proponents of high immigration levels argue that we must retain extended family admission preferences in order to protect family values. Well, let us, remember, Mr. President, that when an immigrant comes to this country, leaving behind parents, brothers, sisters, uncles, aunts and cousins, it is the immigrant who is breaking up the extended family.[25]

Shelby may have had a point, but he sounded defensive and callous, so other senators tried to outdo the proimmigrationists at their own game by claiming that it was *they*, the restrictionists, who were actually profamily. Simpson argued that his bill was more profamily because it preferred the nuclear family over distant relatives who may not have any blood connection. He explained, "We want the nuclear family. We want the number to go to the nuclear family. [The bill] will do that. It will reduce the availability of visas for relatives who are likely to have their own separate households."[26] Representative Smith gave an example to reify the notion that his restrictionist bill was actually profamily. "Today, a 3-year-old little girl and her mother could be separated, a continent away, from the father living in the United States as a legal immigrant. Meanwhile, in the same city, in the same country, we would be admitting a 50-year-old adult brother of a U.S. citizen."[27] Added Representative Bob Goodlatte (R-Va.): "We need to help immediate family members be reunified more quickly. Young married couples with young children, they need to be able to come here more quickly. . . . How do we pay for that? By breaking immigration chains that have very remote connections."[28]

In trying to portray themselves as the "true" profamily supporters, the restrictionists, in essence, ceded intellectual victory to the proimmigrationists. By making the family the crux of the debate, they were operating in an area hostile to their cause and ended up sounding defensive. Despite the restrictionists' insistence that they were the "true" profamily advocates, it took tortured logic to say that somehow reducing family immigration was being "profamily." Though the public supported the restrictionists' view that immigrants had an adverse impact on the economy and culture, the restrictionists were battling in the unfriendly region of family politics, where proimmigrationists had the public support on their side. Once the debate was framed as one over families, proimmigration legislators could act with less fear of a public backlash.

"I'm Not Anti-Family": The Immigration Act of 1990

The Immigration Act of 1990 differed from the 1996 legislation in that it aimed to expand, not reduce, immigration. Despite the diametrically opposed aims, the strategy of using the political rhetoric of the family played a substantial role in the 1990 legislation as well. One lobbyist strategy memo noted that the proimmigrationists need to "secure our control of the intellectual content of the debate. This requires achieving understanding in the media, interest groups and Congress that increased legal immigration will . . . promote *pro-family* and pro-growth values"[29] [emphasis added]. Accordingly, immigration enthusiasts argued that the bill was profamily and that opposition to it was tantamount to opposing family values—an accusation that restrictionists vehemently denied. "I am not anti-family or anti-immigrant," insisted a defensive Senator Alan Simpson during the Judiciary Committee mark-ups.[30]

Immigration supporters worked assiduously to describe the policy of family reunification as consonant with the best traditions of American values. "Keeping nuclear families together is a cornerstone American value. It is a value central to my own concern, and central to this bill," said Representative Bruce Morrison.[31] Or take Representative Joseph Brennan (D-Maine): "Family reunification, one of the bill's highest priorities, reflects the strongest of American values. . . . Let us never forget that this country was built on the stability and strength of the family. . . . Is it inconsistent with our country's principles and ideals to promote or enforce so prolonged a separation of spouses from each other and from their families? We must remedy the heartless deportation of infants, and eliminate the tremendous backlog of families waiting to be reunited."[32]

It was this family rhetoric that justified the adoption of the Hatch-DeConcini amendment, which made the Senate bill's cap "pierceable" by setting a minimum floor of 226,000 for family preference visas. The original Senate bill had included both immediate relatives and family preference visas under a firm ceiling, thus preventing future increases in immigration. The Hatch-DeConcini amendment, for all purposes, eliminated the caps and altered the semirestrictionist thrust of the original bill to an unabashedly proimmigration legislation. Not surprisingly, it had the support of proimmigration representatives and senators. "By setting a cap on family preference visas and continuing, properly to allow unlimited entry to children, spouses and parents, we will be squeezing out brothers and sisters and adult children of naturalized citizens," complained Senator Barbara Milkulski (D-Md.) in calling on her fellow colleagues to support the amendment.[33] In other words, the original Senate bill was anti-family because a rise in immediate relatives could have eaten up visas for other family-preference categories. Though this amendment—by allowing the cap to be "pierced"—had the potential of allowing immigration to increase unabated in future years, senators defended it in the name of the family. Senator Orrin Hatch, in introducing his amendment, argued, "Family reunification under these categories, I believe, is desirable, because it reflects traditional American family values."[34]

Interest groups, especially ethnic groups, used similar "family values" rhetoric to justify the increase in immigration in 1990. "Asian culture, as in many others, holds the family at the highest esteem, providing a support system to its members," said Melinda Yee of the Organization of Chinese Americans.[35] Howard Hom of the Chinese Welfare Council testified, "Everyone would agree that the family unit is the basic building block of human society. Brothers and sisters, whether married or single, whether under 25 or over 25 years old, are integral parts of the family. . . . In your discussions today and in the upcoming vote please keep in mind the importance of the family in American values and tradition."[36] Or take Reverend Joseph A. Cogo of the American Committee on Italian Migration: "Keeping a nuclear family separated for years is a violation of a basic human right."[37] Religious groups also lobbied on behalf of family reunification. "The family can become a fragile and beleaguered institution in a society that gives it no encouragement or support. Family life in the United States is not as healthy as it once was. . . . Given the stress on the American family today, should we add to that stress through our immigration law?" inquired Nicholas DiMarzio of the U.S. Catholic Conference. "What stronger, more enduring basis for an immigration policy is there than the family? The Catholic Church believes that the family is the fundamental building block of society and culture."[38]

Senator Alan Simpson defensively scoffed at the insinuations that he was antifamily. Clearly frustrated by how the debate had been framed by the valence issue of family, Simpson insisted that he "would never be involved in that kind of sinister activity of closing off family immigration. It is so dramatic that it does not ring true."[39] He tried to redirect the focus of the debate away from families and to aggregate numbers. "They must want unlimited immigration into the United States," complained Simpson. But vivid images of families had more emotional resonance than some abstract number, and the thrust of the debate centered on the family.

The Family and the Immigration Reform and Control Act of 1986

Although most of the debate over the IRCA revolved around illegal immigration, the family rhetoric nevertheless played a prominent role in the debate over the legal immigration provisions that capped legal immigration at 425,000 visas and eliminated the existing visa preference for adult siblings of U.S. citizens and for adult children of permanent residents.[40] The provisions were ultimately dropped in the conference agreement in 1984 and never taken up again. The House bill had similar provisions, but they were expunged during the committee mark-ups at the prodding of Peter Rodino (D-N.J.) and various ethnic groups that lobbied hard against them. Repeated attempts to place caps failed during the committee mark-ups. For example, Representative Carlos J. Moorhead's (R-Calif.) amendment for a 450,000 cap was rejected as was Representative James Sensenbrenner's (R-Wis.) amendment to include a flexible cap of 300,000 to 420,000.[41] Moorhead again attempted to place a cap on the floor of Congress but failed.[42]

Immigration enthusiasts argued that subtracting immediate relatives from the family-reunification allotment would force family members to compete against each other for a limited number of visas. Senator Edward Kennedy heralded family reunification as a morally sound system: "It is a proud tradition, a proud part of our heritage, the reunification of families, husbands and wives, fathers and mothers and children, brothers and sisters together."[43] After all, who could be against husbands, fathers, mothers, and children? Others also pointed out that the abolishment of the preference for adult or married children of permanent residents was antifamily in that it arbitrarily denied visas on the sole basis of age. "Simply because a son or daughter reaches 21 he does not leave the nuclear family—especially if he is unmarried," complained Kennedy.[44] "I think it is a good thing for the family unit to be brought together. What we are talking about here are unmarried sons and daughters and parents who wish to [be] reunited with one another and . . . about unmarried brothers and sisters wishing to be reunited with their siblings," pleaded Senator Paul Sarbanes (D-Md.).[45]

His pleas were heeded as Congress scuttled plans to place a firmer cap on legal immigration. The valence issue of family allowed immigration supporters to outmaneuver restrictionist forces and maintain high levels of legal immigration, yet insulate themselves from a potential public backlash. The restrictionists could only watch in frustration.

THE SAVING GRACE OF ILLEGAL IMMIGRATION

Family rhetoric is not the only method that proimmigration enthusiasts have used to defend high levels of immigration amidst hostile public opinion. Fortunately for the proimmigration members of Congress, illegal immigration surged during the 1970s—the same time that legal immigration increased. This coincidence directed the attention of both the public and the policymakers onto illegal immigration. The (mis)perception that the country was being invaded by illegal immigrants allowed proimmigration congressmen—motivated both by interest group pressure and ideological reasons—to cool the public ardor for legal immigration reform by channeling the people's anger toward illegal immigration. It is politically much easier to attack illegal immigrants because, unlike legal immigrants, they do not have powerful interest groups to represent them. In short, Congress could defend its lack of action on legal immigration by passing and touting bills combating illegal immigration.

The restrictionist members of Congress repeatedly tried to link legal and illegal immigration together and address them at the same time in one omnibus bill. But, in the end, many of them realized that powerful proimmigration interest groups could thwart the entire bill, jeopardizing illegal immigration reform in the process. Consequently, many congressional members found it politically expedient to ignore legal immigration and at least get an illegal immigration bill to publicize to their constituents.

The 1996 Debate over Legal and Illegal Immigration

Restrictionist bills like the ones offered in 1996 represent the best case study of the dynamics between illegal and legal immigration. Since the 1996 bills were the only restrictionist bills to receive serious consideration in nearly seventy years, they merit close scrutiny. Representative Lamar Smith's comprehensive immigration reform bill called for a one-third reduction in annual immigration levels. The bill also contained a slew of proposals, ranging from a strengthened Border Patrol to expedited deportation procedures, to combat illegal immigration. The Senate bill by Alan Simpson was similar to Smith's bill. It reduced immigration to 540,000 visas a year and had an illegal immigration component as well.

The proimmigration contingent worked assiduously to distinguish between legal and illegal immigration by praising the former while impugning the latter. Cato Institute's Stephen Moore advised immigration lobbyist Rick Swartz to pursue a strategy of splitting the bill into legal and illegal immigration components: legislators would find it politically expedient to focus on an illegal immigration bill, and the legal immigration reform bill would die. "Our line was that illegal immigration needs to be addressed on its own," said Daphne Kwok of the Organization of Chinese Americans. "We stressed that there is a big difference between legal and illegal immigration, and that distinction has to be made."[46]

Senator Kennedy, who had voted against the 1986 Immigration Reform and Control Act—a bill designed to combat illegal immigration—because he thought it was too draconian, now somewhat disingenuously positioned himself as a hard-line opponent of illegal immigration. He asserted that illegal immigrants "are individuals who violate the laws, effectively take away American jobs, come here unskilled and, in many instances, take scarce taxpayer dollars to support their activities. That is an entirely different profile from those who are legal immigrants. . . . [They] are hard-working people, overwhelmingly successful. They are contributors to our society. We ought to be debating today illegal immigration."[47]

Other senators repeated this theme ad nauseum. Senator Barbara Boxer (D-Calif.), for example, said, "There is a real difference between illegal immigration and legal immigration." Representative Nancy Pelosi (D-Calif.) added, "I agree with my colleagues that we must curb illegal immigration responsibly and effectively. However, as the Berman, Brownback and Chrysler amendment recognizes, the issue of legal immigration is clearly distinct and separate."[48] Or Representative Jay Kim (R-Calif.):

Illegal aliens have knowingly and willingly violated the law by entering the United States without permission. They defraud the taxpayer. On the contrary, legal immigrants have patiently waited, paid all the requisite fees and deposits, and followed all the rules and regulations for resettling in the United States. They will soon be proud, patriotic citizens. . . . Thus, to consider the status of these two, totally opposite groups in the same bill is both unfair and an insult to legal immigrants.[49]

And Representative Howard Berman (D-Calif.) put it this way: "I think it is fundamentally wrong to take the justifiable anger about our failure to deal with the issue of illegal immigration and piggyback on top of that anger, a drastic, in 5 years 40 percent cut in permanent legal immigration, a cause and a force that has been good for this country."[50]

Some proimmigration legislators defended their unpopular stance on legal immigration by contrasting it with their popular hard-line position against illegal immigration. "I do not believe we have a legal immigration problem. Illegal immigrants are lawbreakers. They are lawbreakers. And no country can exist unless it enforces its laws. We absolutely have to do that. Legal immigrants, on the other hand, are by and large great citizens. They are people who care about their families. They are people who work hard," claimed Senator Mike DeWine (R-Ohio), insinuating that illegal immigrants do not work hard or care about their families.[51] That implication is rather deceptive:

most illegal immigrants work hard and do care for their families. They enter America illegally because Congress created such a Byzantine and often illogical policy that encourages illegal immigration. But Senator DeWine later proudly said in a statement tailor-made for his constituents: "I voted for tough penalties for those who violate our immigration laws, and I voted to expedite the deportation of those violators."[52]

Senator Spencer Abraham (R-Mich.) used the same tactic as that of DeWine. Abraham's split-the-bill amendment in the Judiciary Committee had killed legal immigration reform by separating the legal and illegal immigration provisions. Although he may be generous toward legal immigration, Abraham made it clear that he absolutely opposes illegal immigration. Senator Alan Simpson notes that Abraham "really stepped up the heat on illegal immigration once they [proimmigrationists] killed off legal immigration because they felt a bit guilty—that we're going to have a million people coming instead of 500,000—so Spencer Abraham put up the toughest and strongest legislation on illegal immigration."[53] Indeed, Abraham offered several successful committee amendments that increased border patrol by 300 officers, imposed a forced waiting period of at least three years for visa overstayers who apply for another visa, and established expedited deportation procedures for illegal aliens.[54] The harshness toward illegal immigration allowed legislators like Abraham who support legal immigration to defuse any potential backlash from their constituents by pointing to their leadership against illegal immigration.

This tactic was transparent to restrictionists. "As I say, this is a plenty tough package. Everyone should be able to appropriately thump their chest when they get back to the old home district and say, 'Boy, did we do a number on illegals in this country,' " noted Senator Simpson sarcastically.[55] Representative John Bryant (D-Tex.) perceptively observed that we "have a bunch of Members going around there beating their breasts, talking about how tough they got on illegal immigrants, but they avoided the tough question where the interest groups are putting the pressure on everybody; that is, the question of legal immigrants."[56] Added Skip Garling of FAIR: "Everyone loves to concentrate on illegal immigration—they say they're lawbreakers—but that's a red herring. What they're doing with illegal immigration won't solve the problem because three times as many legal immigrants as there are illegal. They just tackle the politically easy issue of illegal immigration."[57] Representative Bryant, though no friend of illegal immigration, was offended by the bidding war to outdo each other in the hopes of appearing tough against illegal immigration. In reference to a "one-strike and you're out" amendment for illegal aliens, Bryant complained, "This is a press release, OK? This is not an amendment. This is a press release. So you folks can write letters and say, 'Oh, boy, I got tough on illegal immigration.' "[58]

Restrictionists tried vainly to link legal and illegal immigration, drawing similarities between the two. "If you are talking about reducing immigration, you cannot just talk about illegal immigration," argued Senator Simpson.[59] Senator Richard Shelby (R-Ala.) went for the jugular in linking the two:

> Legal immigration is also linked to illegal immigration because it has many of the same impacts. Both legal and illegal immigration involve large numbers of additional people, with legal in fact accounting for nearly three times more new U.S. residents than illegal immigration. Many of my colleagues have expressed grave concerns about illegal immigrants taking jobs from Americans, or these immigrants committing crimes or costing taxpayers and State and local governments millions for public education, welfare and other public assistance. . . . It is time to recognize that legal immigrants often cause these same types of adverse impacts. Congress must stop overlooking or disregarding this patently obvious fact. Let there be no mistake we will not solve most of our national immigration problem by just dealing with illegal immigration. Legal immigration is in many ways an even greater part of the problem.[60]

Despite this plea by Senator Shelby, Congress decide to kill legal immigration reform and only act on illegal immigration. The coalition of conservatives and liberals proved too strong for the restrictionists. Sheer political expediency also played a big role. It was much easier to act against illegal immigrants than to tackle the entrenched legal immigration lobby. Many legislators who actually favored legal immigration reform in the end supported splitting the bill into legal and illegal parts because they needed something—an illegal immigration law—to show to their constituents come election time. In one salient example, ten Californian Republicans wrote a letter to their colleagues, reluctantly urging them to divide the bill. They feared that legal immigration provisions were "resulting in the further delay of needed efforts to stop illegal immigration."[61] As Paul Mero, the chief of staff of Representative Bob Dornan (R-Calif.), put it, "Illegal immigration is such an important issue to Southern California. You tie it up with the issue of legal immigration and you give cover to the Democrats to beat the whole bill to a pulp."[62]

The Legal and Illegal Linkage in Other Bills

Although the Immigration Act of 1990 was not a restrictionist bill, it nevertheless showed some of the similar legal-illegal immigration dynamics.

The final Senate version of the Immigration Act of 1990 included a 630,000 pierceable cap with a minimum floor of 226,000 for family-reunification visas. Overall, the bill would have increased immigration and was generally proimmigration. The House offered an even more generous immigration bill by giving unlimited visas for spouses and minor children of permanent U.S residents. The total national level under the House bill would have come in at around 800,000.

Appalled by the House bill's nearly 60% increase in visas, Senator Simpson threatened to delay and kill the bill. "I've let bills die before," he ominously warned.[63] He demanded a lower and firmer ceiling on immigration. Simpson particularly stressed the importance of a firm cap to ensure that immigration would not unexpectedly spike up in the future. Simpson wanted no more than a total of 675,000 immigrants to come annually. After intense negotiating, conferees ultimately came to a compromise. Simpson dropped his demands for a firm cap: the final bill set the cap at 700,000 for the first three years and 675,000 thereafter, but that ceiling was in fact no ceiling at all because it could be easily pierced if the number of immediate relatives increased. In return for this concession, Simpson received an array of provisions combating illegal immigration. The bill included stronger border patrol, a pilot program to create forgery-proof identifications that could be used by employers to ferret out illegal immigrants, expedited deportation procedures, and civil penalties for document fraud.[64] Simpson and other restrictionists rationalized that a stiffer legal immigration bill had no chance of passage, so they decided to get at least something, that is, tougher illegal immigration provisions.

The Immigration Reform and Control Act is different from the 1990 and 1996 laws in that proimmigrationists did not use illegal immigration provisions as a way to shield themselves from public opinion or to win concessions from restrictionists. In fact, the major thrust of the bill started out as an anti-illegal immigration bill. What it does show, however, is how the entrenched interest group activity in the legal immigration policy network makes it enticing even for restrictionists to tackle illegal, instead of legal, immigration reform.

The original bill for the Immigration Reform and Control Act addressed both illegal and legal immigration. In addition to employer sanctions and an amnesty program, Senator Alan Simpson proposed capping legal immigration at 425,000 visas. The visas for numerically exempt immediate relatives of United States citizens would have been subtracted from the total allotment for family reunification. The bill also eliminated the existing visa preference for adult siblings of U.S. citizens, and denied visas for adult children of permanent residents.

Senator Simpson at first tried to lump both illegal and legal immigration together. "Poll after poll discloses that the American people overwhelmingly wish to see both illegal and legal immigration under control. In these past several years I have wanted to discover the significance of this fact and I have learned that their concern is well founded," said Simpson in pushing for his bill.[65] Others contested Simpson's assertion, drawing stark contrasts between legal and illegal immigration. "Yes, illegal immigration must be controlled. But there is no evidence that the current levels of legal immigration are dangerous or contrary to our national interest," said Senator Edward Kennedy.[66]

Even those who wanted reductions in the number of legal immigrants spent most of their time on illegal immigration because they and their constituents considered illegal immigration to be the top priority. As Senator Lawton Chiles (D-Fla.) put it, "While legal immigration is a serious problem, illegal immigration presents an even more serious problem."[67] Senator Simpson eventually agreed. Simpson had included both legal and illegal immigration provisions in his bill in both 1982 and 1984, but the legal immigration section, amid intense lobbying and strife, was removed in the conference agreement in 1984. Senator Simpson, realizing how many interest groups opposed legal reform and fearing this might jeopardize the entire bill, did not even bother including legal immigration reform in his bill in 1986. "One of the lessons that Simpson learned was that less is more," noted Rick Swartz. "If you try to do less, you'll get more accomplished because the more comprehensive your bill, the more enemies you'll create."[68]

It would not be a far stretch to say that the best ally of legal immigrants are illegal immigrants. The sudden increase in illegal immigration during the 1970s had a dual effect: it not only dwarfed legal immigration in the policy agenda but it also allowed proimmigration legislators to attack illegal immigration as a tactic to "save" legal immigration. It insulated proimmigration legislators from potential public backlash for their votes against legal immigration reform, because they could at least point to the harsh measures against illegal immigration as a symbol of their determination to "get tough." This was best seen in the 1996 bills. Public opinion runs high against legal immigration but much more so against illegal immigration. So proim-migrationists shrewdly diverted attention toward illegal immigrants, who are universally detested and have little interest group repre-sentation. Then they could go back home to their districts and tell their constituents of the recently passed illegal immigration bill.

Likewise in 1990, proimmigration legislators traded harsh sanctions against illegal immigrants in order to win a more generous legal immigration policy. And in the Immigration Reform and Control Act, restrictionists were deterred from legal immigration reform without any prodding from proimmigrationists—it was politically foolish to endanger a politically popular illegal immigration bill by including a legal immigration provision in it. In all three of these cases, illegal immigration helped "save" legal immigration.

NOTES

1. Eric Schmitt, "In Immigration Bill Debate, Divisions and Odd Alli-ances," *New York Times*, 26 February 1996, p. A1.

2. According to a poll, a 1997 Houston ballot proposition to eradicate affirmative action had the support of 68.1% of city residents (and opposed by 16.1%) when it was worded as, "The City of Houston shall not discriminate against or grant preferential treatment to any individual or group on the basis of race, sex, ethnicity, or national origin in the operation of public employ-ment and public contracting." The proposition's phrasing, however, was changed by the mayor to the city shall "end the use of affirmative action for women and minorities." Under this new phrasing, the ballot initiative lost 54% to 46%. See Sam Howe Verhovek, "Houston to Vote on Repeal of Affirmative Action," *New York Times*, 2 November 1997, p. A28.

3. Keith Fitzgerald, *The Face of the Nation: Immigration, the State and the National Identity* (Stanford, Calif.: Stanford University Press, 1996), p. 234.

4. U.S. Congress, House Committee on Immigration and Naturalization, *Japanese Immigration: Hearings*, 66th Congress, 2d Session, 1921, p. 1384.

5. See George Borjas, *Friends or Strangers: The Impact of Immigration on the U.S. Economy* (New York: Basic Books, 1990), and Vernon Briggs, Jr., *Mass Immigration and the National Interest* (Armonk, N.Y.: M. E. Sharpe, 1992) for a less optimistic view of immigration. See Julian Simon, *The Economic Consequences of Immigration* (New York: B. Blackwell, 1989) for a proimmigration view.

6. U.S. Congress, House Subcommittee on Immigration, Refugees and International Law, and Immigration Task Force of the Committee on Educa-

tion and Labor, *Immigration Act of 1989 (Part 3): Hearings*, 101st Congress, 2d session, 1989, pp. 308–9.

7. Ibid., p. 8.

8. Ibid., p. 82.

9. Ibid., p. 84.

10. Kenneth Lee, "Rebel Children," *American Enterprise*, September/October 1997, p. 30.

11. Barbara Dafoe Whitehead, "Dan Quayle Was Right," *Atlantic Monthly*, April 1993, p. 47.

12. For example, see Margaret Talbot, "Love, American Style," *New Republic*, 14 April 1997, p. 30.

13. Interviewed by author, April 2, 1997.

14. *Congressional Record*, 20 March 1996, pp. H2536–37.

15. Ibid., p. H2596.

16. Ibid., p. H2597.

17. *Congressional Record*, 15 April 1996, p. S3296 and p. S4127.

18. Ibid., p. S4140.

19. House Subcommittee, *Immigration Act of 1989 (Part 3)*, p. 215–16.

20. Ibid., p. 287.

21. U.S. Congress, House Subcommittee on Immigration and Claims, *Immigration in the National Interest Act of 1995: Hearings*, 104th Congress, 1st Session, 1995, p. 194.

22. Interviewed by author, April 2, 1997.

23. House Subcommittee, *Immigration in the National Interest Act of 1995*, p. 194.

24. Interviewed by author, March 31, 1997.

25. *Congressional Record*, 25 April 1996, pp. S4129–30.

26. Ibid., p. S4119.

27. *Congressional Record*, 21 March 1996, p. H2590.

28. Ibid., p. H2598.

29. Memorandum, June 23, 1990, papers from the Office of Rick Swartz & Associates.

30. U.S. Congress, Senate, *Immigration Act of 1989*, Senate Report 101–55, p. 79.

31. *Congressional Record*, 2 October 1990, p. H8638.

32. Ibid., p. H8648.

33. *Congressional Record*, 13 July 1989, p. S14564.

34. *Congressional Record*, 12 July 1989, p. S14298.

35. U.S. Congress, House Subcommittee on Immigration, Refugees and International Law, *Immigration Act of 1989 (Part 1): Hearings*, 101st Congress, 1st Session, 1989, p. 244.

36. Ibid., p. 289.

37. Ibid., p. 258.

38. Ibid., pp. 293, 310–11.

39. *Congressional Record*, 13 July 1989, p. S14304.

40. "Immigration Reform Measure Dies in House," *1982 Congressional Quarterly Almanac*, p. 407.

41. Nadine Cohodas, "Immigration Reform Measure Approved by House Judiciary," *Congressional Quarterly Weekly Report*, 7 May 1983, p. 913.

42. "Immigration Reform Dies at Session's End," *1984 Congressional Quarterly Almanac*, p. 232.

43. *Congressional Record*, 12 August 1982, p. S20835.

44. Ibid., p. S20850.

45. Ibid., p. S20853.

46. Interviewed by author, April 2, 1997.

47. *Congressional Record*, 25 April 1996, p. S4120.

48. *Congressional Record*, 21 March 1996, p. H2601.

49. Ibid., p. H2602.

50. Ibid., p. H2591.

51. *Congressional Record*, 25 April 1996, p. S4126.

52. Ibid., p. S4126.

53. Interviewed by author, April 11, 1997.

54. U.S Congress, Senate Judiciary Committee Report, *Immigration Control and Financial Responsibility Act of 1996*, 104th Congress, 2d Session, 1996, S. Rept. 104–249, pp. 40–41.

55. *Congressional Record*, 30 April 1996, p. S4377.

56. *Congressional Record*, 21 March 1996, p. H2592.

57. Interviewed by author, April 11, 1997.

58. *Congressional Record*, 19 March 1996, p. S2459.

59. *Congressional Record*, 25 April 1996, p. S4120.

60. Ibid., p. S4130.

61. Steven Holmes, "House Republicans May Split Immigration Bill to Keep It from Bogging Down," *New York Times*, 2 November 1995, p. B10.

62. Ibid., p. B10.

63. Joan Biskupic, "Simpson Holds Bill Hostage, Major Changes," *Congressional Quarterly Weekly Report*, 13 October 1990, p. 3424.

64. Joan Biskupic, "Sizable Boost in Immigration OK'd in Compromise Bill," *Congressional Quarterly Weekly Report*, 27 October 1990, p. 3609.

65. *Congressional Record*, 17 August 1982, p. S21665.

66. *Congressional Record*, 12 August 1982, p. S20834.

67. Ibid., p. S20840.

68. Interviewed by author, April 2, 1997.

Chapter 8

Prospects for the Future

When Representative Lamar Smith and Senator Alan Simpson introduced their restrictionist bills in the 104th Congress, legal immigration
reform seemed almost inevitable. Public discontent over the post-1965
immigration policy had hit its apogee as polls revealed that about
two-thirds of Americans wanted to reduce immigration levels. The
political climate seemed propitious for restrictionist legislation. The
Commission on Immigration Reform, chaired by the respected former
Congresswoman Barbara Jordan, recommended that legal immigration
be reduced by one-third. The final report carried considerable weight
among policymakers because of the commission's distinguished membership. President Bill Clinton—always eager to pander to voters,
especially those in electoral-rich California—heartily endorsed the Jordan commission's recommendations. Among the Republicans, Pat
Buchanan rode to victory in several states during the 1996 primary
season by pillorying immigrants. The eventual Republican presidential
candidate, Bob Dole, did not stoop to Buchanan's xenophobic popu-
lism, but he endorsed the commission's recommendations.

And with Simpson and Smith chairing the immigration subcommittees in Congress, virtually all the political pundits and prognosticators
believed that the United States would enact the first restrictionist
legislation since the 1920s. If legal immigration reform was ever going
to be enacted in the near future, it was to be in 1996. But that did not

happen. The legal immigration bills foundered in Congress, and only a modest illegal immigration bill was passed as an attachment to a larger appropriations bill.

Prospects for immigration reform in the near future seem bleak. Representative Smith says that he will not pursue a comprehensive immigration legislation in the immediate future.[1] Alan Simpson, the leading restrictionist voice in the Senate for the past two decades, retired in 1996, and his immigration subcommittee chair has been filled by Senator Spencer Abraham, an ardent immigration enthusiast. The congressional leadership is also reluctant to tackle immigration reform. "I really don't see much prospects of more action in that area, at least not this year," Senate majority leader Trent Lott reassured the United States Chamber of Commerce.[2]

Yet the public discontent over high levels of immigration has not abated. According to a *Wall Street Journal* poll conducted in December 1996, 72% want immigration to be curbed.[3] In 1965, only one-third had called for reductions. Historically, public policy has generally followed public opinion on the issue of immigration. When nativist fever hit its peak during the 1920s, Congress enacted the National Origins Acts to curtail immigration drastically. By the 1960s, when anti-immigrant attitudes had declined, public policy shifted again and Congress abolished the national origins system. Yet, public policy has not reflected public opinion since the enactment of the seminal 1965 Immigration Act.

This brief book has tried to explain why this divergence has existed for the past thirty years. Fortuitous historical circumstances have increased the power of expansionists vis-à-vis the restrictionists and have facilitated an unusual proimmigration coalition of conservative and liberal interest groups and politicians. First, the civil rights movement greatly weakened the racialistic arguments that had historically provided a powerful impetus for restrictions. Most nativist groups that had previously dominated public policy had disappeared by the 1960s or were considered pariahs. At the same time, ethnic groups became an important force in the Democratic party. These developments solidified the proimmigration sentiment on the Left side of the coalition.

The other important historical change was the ascendancy of conservative economics in a rapidly globalizing economy during the late 1970s. As the United States began to lose its competitive edge to upstarts like Japan and Germany, laissez-faire ideologues stressed the importance of low taxes, minimal government regulation, and free trade in a global economy. Part of this free-market vision included an open immigration policy, which would allow the free flow of people across borders. Conservatives argued that immigrants could reinvigorate American competitiveness by attracting the best and the brightest from the world. As Yale law professor Peter Schuck argues, the power of ideas should not be discounted in recent immigration legislation.[4]

Just as important was the logrolling strategy and the avoidance of zero-sum politics. Instead of competing against each other for a finite number of visas, business groups and ethnic organizations decided to work together to expand visas for everyone. So Congress in 1990 ended up expanding both skills-based and family-reunification visas, and, in 1996, the Left-Right coalition worked to defeat reductions in both areas.

Though the powerful coalition of conservative interest groups and liberal lobbyists explains the influence of organized interests on public policy, it does not fully explain how Congress can afford to ignore the public opinion. Proimmigrationists have discovered two key ways to blunt the hostile public opinion on immigration. First, they have redirected the public anger toward illegal immigration in hopes of "saving" legal immigration. Illegal immigration spiked up in the 1970s—the same time that legal immigration increased—drawing attention away from legal immigration. By acting tough on illegal immigration, they have partially shielded themselves from criticisms that they are doing nothing about immigration. In 1986, 1990, and 1996, proimmigration legislators managed to scuttle restrictionist legal immigration reform and, instead, enact illegal immigration legislation. Second, proimmigrationists have ingeniously reshaped the terms of the debate by focusing on the family, not on abstract numbers. Virtually all Americans consider the family to be sacrosanct, and they are more supportive of immigration if they are given heart-rending scenarios of immigrant families being separated. Immigration enthusiasts insulated themselves from potential public backlash by casting themselves as profamily and their opponents as antifamily.

THE FUTURE

Legal immigration reform seems unlikely in the near future, but what about twenty or thirty years from now? Although political prognostications should be taken with a grain of salt, it seems unlikely that we will enact any drastic legal immigration reform in the next few decades.

The same factors that have precluded such reform for the past thirty years will continue to be in play in the next few decades. The economy will continue to globalize, and it will force countries to adopt more free-market policies in order to remain competitive with other nations. It seems unlikely that legal immigration will be drastically limited in an era of free trade and free markets. As proimmigrationists point out, nearly one-third of the engineers in Silicon Valley are foreign-born, and these immigrants provide the United States with tremendous human capital at little cost.

Secondly, recrudescent racism seems just as unlikely. Most Americans, especially the younger generation, eschew the nativist rhetoric that was so effectively used in the early twentieth century. Although there is a backlash against affirmative action and preferential treatment, there are few signs that most Americans reject the central tenets of the civil rights movement: equality before the law. One cannot consider today's opposition to affirmative action as tantamount to resurgent racism. There are some signs that many people do fear a "browning" of America, but it is yet to be seen if this fear will transform itself into the virulent nativism of yesteryears.

Furthermore, the problem of illegal immigration remains largely unsolved, despite legislative attempts (e.g., the Immigration Reform and Control Act of 1986) and a draconian state ballot proposition in California (Proposition 187). In fact, the problem seems to have gotten worse. In 1987, the illegal alien population had hit an all-time high of 6 million, but that number decreased as the Immigration Reform and Control Act went into effect.[5] More recently, government officials had believed that around 4 million people resided in the United States illegally. However, in 1997, the Immigration and Naturalization Service reported that the illegal alien population had begun creeping upwards again and had reached 5 million.[6] The INS report, the most comprehensive government study of its kind, also said that the illegal immigration population was continuing to increase at an annual rate of 275,000. California, in particular, served as a haven for illegal immigrants. According to the INS, about 6.3% of the California population was undocumented.[7] This continuing problem allows proimmigration legislators to shield themselves from public backlash by continuing to concentrate their efforts on illegal immigration.

Furthermore, the politics of family has firmly entrenched itself into the American polity. There is a virtual consensus among both Republicans and Democrats that the American family is in a precarious situation: nearly half the marriages end in divorce, illegitimate births continue to skyrocket, teenage pregnancies remain high, and so forth. As long as "family-values" remain a part of our political parlance, proimmigration legislators will continue to defend their immigration views by standing behind the banner of the family.

There are some trends, however, that indicate that the elite opinion on immigration might be slightly shifting toward the restrictionist end of the political spectrum. A 321–page RAND Corporation study released in September 1997 recommended a moderate reduction in immigration, arguing that high levels of unskilled immigration exacerbated unemployment, especially in California. "There appears to be a growing divergence between current trends in the state's economy and immigration policies that are producing a steady inflow of poorly educated immigrants," said the report.[8] The Rand study received scathing attacks from immigration enthusiasts. "This sounds like think tank poppycock," said Frank Sharry of the National Immigration Forum. "It's smart people thinking that the only thing the country needs is more smart people."[9] Added Gregory Rodriguez, a research fellow at Pepperdine University's Institute for Public Policy, "It's saying we don't want striving people anymore."[10]

Only four months before, the National Research Council had promulgated a voluminous 500-page federally funded study on immigration. The study, which took two years to finish and was subjected to academic peer review, offered a mixed portrait of immigration. It stated that immigrants added a net plus of $10 billion into the American economy each year, but also noted that immigration displaced low-skilled native workers and posed an unfair fiscal burden on California.[11] Both critics and supporters of immigration hailed the study as supporting their cause. "This confirms the generally critical view that immigration is a policy that enriches those who have and takes away from those who have not," said Mark Krikorian of the Center for Immigration Studies, a restrictionist group.[12] Citing the same study, Cecilia Munoz of the National Council of La Raza said, "This should put to rest a lot of the more irresponsible studies published by anti-immigrant groups and demonstrate that by and large this country has benefited from its generous tradition of welcoming immigrants."[13] The RAND Corporation and National Research Council studies reveal that some academics and policymakers are inching toward the restrictionist camp, but the empirical evidence is still too mixed to mark a discernible change in elite opinion on immigration.

An unexpected crisis situation in the future can, of course, lead to reductions in immigration. For example, a severe depression may prompt some policymakers to seek cuts in immigration. A more likely scenario is that immigration will remain high for the foreseeable future, but there will be attempts to reduce the fiscal and social costs of immigration. The welfare reform passed by the Republican Congress and signed by President Bill Clinton is a salient example of how immigration will be indirectly addressed in the future. The welfare law allowed states to eliminate Aid to Families with Dependent Children (AFDC), Supplemental Security Income (SSI) and other social welfare programs for many legal immigrants.[14] The left wing of the Left-Right coalition protested these welfare changes as callous, but the right-leaning members openly embraced them as a way to cut costs and discourage the less competitive immigrants from coming to the United States. Without the help of the conservative faction of the Left-Right coalition, liberal groups lost. These changes in welfare policy only underscore the importance of the Left-Right coalition in maintaining high levels of immigration.

Similarly, the backlash against multiculturalism and bilingualism can be seen as a method to mitigate the social costs of immigration. Granted, some nativists mask their parochial views in opposing multiculturalism. But, for the most part, sensible and fair people oppose multiculturalism because of the legitimate fear that the more radical and anti-American elements of multiculturalism will further balkanize our already fragmented national culture. In fact, the most incisive critique of multiculturalism and bilingualism to date has come not from the Right but rather from the Left: the venerable liberal historian Arthur Schlesinger wrote a powerful polemic, *The Disuniting of America*, excoriating the new trend of identity-politics. We can expect more resistance to multiculturalism and bilingualism in the future. Most recently, virtually every member of the Senate censured the National History Standards as multicultural nonsense. It was originally conceived to establish a national standard of basic history that all competent grade school students should be familiar with, but as editorialists have repeatedly pointed out, the proposed standards, in an attempt to be more multicultural, downplayed the seminal roles played by white males like George Washington and Thomas Edison, while they uncritically eulogized the Aztecs and Indians.[15] And in California, voters voted to eliminate bilingual education in public schools by a 2-to-1 margin in a recent state proposition.

These battles over multiculturalism and welfare are nothing new. Even in the late nineteenth century, social critics passionately debated the assimilability and the fiscal costs of immigrants. That immigration will broach such acrimonious issues is not unexpected: immigration, unlike many other forms of public policy, has the power literally to change the face of the nation. And such a momentous change should require a thorough and judicious debate.

NOTES

1. Interviewed by author, March 31, 1997.

2. Eric Schmitt, "Effort to Reduce Legal Immigration Loses Impetus in Congress," *New York Times*, 17 January 1997, p. A17.

3. *Wall Street Journal*, December 13, 1996, p. R4.

4. Peter Schuck, "The Politics of Rapid Legal Change: Immigration Policy in the 1980s," Marc K. Landy and Martin A. Levin, eds., *The New Politics of Public Policy* (Baltimore: Johns Hopkins University Press, 1995), p. 50–51.

5. Patrick J. McDonnell, "Illegal Immigrant Population in U.S. Now Tops 5 Million," *Los Angeles Times*, 8 February 1997, p. A1.

6. Ibid., p. A1.

7. Ibid., p. A1.

8. Patrick J. McDonnell, "Immigration Study Urges New Curbs and Criteria," *Los Angeles Times*, 15 September 1997, p. A1. The Rand study also recommended applying education levels and English proficiency as factors in determining admission.

9. Ibid., p. A1.

10. Ibid., p. A1.

11. Patrick J. McDonnell, "Immigrants a Net Economic Plus, Study Says," *Los Angeles Times*, 18 May 1997, p. A3.

12. Ibid., p. A3.

13. Ibid., p. A3.

14. Most of these changes were reversed and social welfare benefits were restored for immigrants when President Bill Clinton and the Republican Congress agreed on a budget compromise.

15. Walter A. McDougall, "What Johnny Still Won't Know about History," *Commentary*, July 1996, pp. 32–36.

Selected Bibliography

This is only a selective bibliography; it contains the sources that I found most helpful in my research. Of these, Keith Fitzgerald's book *The Face of a Nation*, Peter Schuck's chapter "The Politics of Rapid Legal Change: Immigration Policy in the 1980s," and Daniel J. Tichenor's article "The Politics of Immigration Reform in the United States, 1981–1990" were most insightful in discussing the coalition politics of recent immigration reform. Also shown below is a partial listing of interviewed people who patiently provided incisive analysis and details on recent immigration politics.

ARTICLES AND BOOKS

"Ambivalence toward Immigration." *American Enterprise.* March/April 1995: 105.

Anderson, James E. *Public Policy-Making.* New York: Praeger, 1975.

Applebome, Peter. "Surge of Illegal Aliens Taxes Southwest Towns' Resources." *New York Times,* 9 March 1986: 1.

Arnold, R. Douglas. "Can Citizens Control Their Representatives?" *Congress Reconsidered.* Lawrence C. Dodd and Bruce I. Oppenheimer, eds. Washington, D.C.: Congressional Quarterly Press, 1993.

———. *The Logic of Congressional Action.* New Haven: Yale University Press, 1990.

Auster, Lawrence. *The Path to National Suicide: An Essay on Immigration and Multiculturalism.* Monterey, Calif.: The American Immigration Control Foundation, 1990.

Bean, Frank D., Barry Edmonston, and Jeffrey S. Passel, eds. *Undocumented Migration to the United States: IRCA and the Experience of the 1980s.* Washington, D.C.: Urban Institute Press, 1990.

Bean, Frank D., Georges Vernez, and Charles B. Keely. *Opening and Closing the Doors: Evaluating Immigration Reform and Control.* Washington, D.C.: Urban Institute Press, 1989.

Bernstein, Richard. "For Ellis Island, A Reborn Role as a Monument." *New York Times,* 9 December 1982: B1.

Bernstein, Robert A. *Elections, Representation, and Congressional Voting Behavior: The Myth of Constituency Control.* Englewood Cliffs, N.J.: Prentice Hall, 1989.

"Bill to Curb Illegal Immigration: House Debate Reflects Diversity of Nation." *New York Times,* 17 June 1984: 21.

Binkley, Wilfred E. *American Political Parties: Their Natural History.* New York: Alfred A. Knopf, 1945.

Biskupic, Joan. "Simpson Holds Bill Hostage, Major Changes." *Congressional Quarterly Weekly Report,* 13 October 1990: 3424.

———. "Sizable Boost in Immigration OK'd in Compromise Bill." *Congressional Quarterly Weekly Report,* 27 October 1990: 3609.

Borjas, George. *Friends or Strangers: The Impact of Immigration on the U.S. Economy.* New York: Basic Books, 1990.

Brand, David. "The New Whiz Kids: Why Asian Americans Are Doing So Well, and What It Costs Them." *Time,* 31 August 1987: 42–48.

Briggs, Vernon M., Jr. *Immigration Policy and the American Labor Force.* Baltimore: Johns Hopkins University Press, 1984.

———. *Mass Immigration and the National Interest.* Armonk, N.Y.: M. E. Sharpe, Inc., 1992.

Brimelow, Peter. *Alien Nation: Common Sense about America's Immigration Disaster.* New York: Random House, 1995.

Brodie, Fawn M. *Thomas Jefferson: An Intimate History.* New York: W. W. Norton & Company, 1974.

Campbell, Tina A. "Immigration Law: The Role of the Supreme Court in Policy Development." *New England Law Review* 22 (1987): 131–63.

Carney, Dan. "As White House Calls Shots, Illegal Alien Bill Clears." *Congressional Quarterly Weekly Report,* 5 October 1996: 2864.

Chiswick, Barry, ed. *The Gateway: U.S. Immigration Issues and Policies.* Washington, D.C.: The American Enterprise Institute, 1982.

Cobb, Roger, Jennie-Keith Ross, and Marc Howard Ross. "Agenda Building as a Comparative Political Process." *American Political Science Review* 70 (1976): 126.

Cohodas, Nadine. "Immigration Reform Measure Approved by House Judiciary." *Congressional Quarterly Weekly Report*, 7 May 1983: 913.

———. "Senate Passes Immigration Reform Bill." *Congressional Quarterly Weekly Report*, 21 May 1983: 1006.

Congressional Record. 1982–1996.

Cook, Timothy E. *Making Laws and Making News: Media Strategies in the U.S. House of Representatives*. Washington, D.C.: The Brookings Institution, 1989.

Crewdson, John M. "Illegal Aliens are Bypassing Farms for Higher Pay of Jobs in the Cities." *New York Times*, 10 November 1980: A1.

Dahl, Robert. *Who Governs?* New Haven: Yale University Press, 1961.

Davidson, Roger H., and Walter J. Oleszek. *Congress and Its Members*. Washington, D.C.: Congressional Quarterly Press, 1994.

Deering, Christopher J., ed. *Congressional Politics*. Chicago: The Dorsey Press, 1989.

Dodd, Lawrence C., and Bruce I. Oppenheimer, eds. *Congress Reconsidered*. Washington, D.C.: Congressional Quarterly Press, 1993.

Down, Anthony. "Up and Down with Ecology: The Issue-Attention Cycle." David L. Protess and Maxwell McCombs, eds. *Agenda Setting: Readings on Media, Public Opinion and Policymaking*. Hillsdale, N.J.: Erlbaum, 1991.

Dye, Thomas R. *Who's Running America? The Clinton Years*. Englewood Cliffs, N.J.: Prentice Hall, 1995.

Edmonston, Barry, Jeffrey S. Passel, and Frank D. Bean, "Perceptions and Estimates of Undocumented Migration to the United States." Frank D. Bean, Barry Edmonston, and Jeffrey S. Passel, eds. *Undocumented Migration to the United States: IRCA and the Experience of the 1980s*. Washington, D.C.: Urban Institute, 1990.

Fitzgerald, Keith. *The Face of the Nation: Immigration, the State and the National Identity*. Stanford, Calif.: Stanford University Press, 1996.

Flint, Peter B. "Rise Seen in Pay to Illegal Aliens in State." *New York Times*, 22 February 1975: 58.

Frisch, Morton, ed. *The Selected Writings and Speeches of Alexander Hamilton*. Washington, D.C.: The American Enterprise Institute, 1985.

Fuchs, Lawrence H. "The Search for a Sound Immigration Policy: A Personal View," Nathan Glazer, ed. *Clamor at the Gates*. San Francisco: ICS Press, 1985.

Garry, Patrick M. *Liberalism and American Identity*. Kent, Ohio: The Kent State University Press, 1992.

Gilder, George. *Spirit of Enterprise*. New York: Simon & Schuster, 1984.

———. *Wealth and Poverty*. New York: Basic Books, 1981.

Glazer, Nathan, ed. *Clamor at the Gates: The New American Immigration*. San Francisco: ICS Press, 1985.

Gobel, Thomas. "Becoming American: Ethnic Workers and the Rise of the CIO." George E. Pozzetta, ed. *Unions and Immigrants: Organization and Struggle.* New York: Garland Publishing, 1991.

Gurwitt, Rob, and Nadine Cohodas. "Hispanic-Asian Boycott: A Gesture Fizzles." *Congressional Quarterly Weekly Report,* 21 July 1984: 1733.

Hartz, Louis. *The Liberal Tradition in America.* San Diego: Harcourt Brace Jovanovich, 1983.

Harwood, Edwin. "American Public Opinion and U.S. Immigration Policy." *Annals of the American Academy of Political and Social Sciences* 487 (1986): 201–12.

Higham, John. *Strangers in the Land: Patterns of American Nativism: 1860–1925.* New Brunswick, N.J.: Rutgers University Press, 1955.

Hoefer, Michael D. "Background on U.S. Immigration Policy Reform." Francisco L. Rivera-Batiz, Selig L. Sechzer, and Ira N. Gang, eds. *U.S. Immigration Policy Reform in the 1980s: A Preliminary Assessment.* New York: Praeger, 1991.

Hofstetter, Richard R., ed. *U.S. Immigration Policy.* Durham, N.C.: Duke University Press, 1984.

Holloway, Harry, and John George. *Public Opinion: Coalitions, Elites and Masses.* 2d ed. New York: St. Martin's Press, 1986.

Holmes, Steven. "House Republicans May Split Immigration Bill to Keep It from Bogging Down." *New York Times,* 2 November 1995: B10.

Idelson, Holly. "Business Lobbies Fighting Foreign Worker Curbs." *Congressional Quarterly Weekly Report,* 25 November 1995: 3600–3601.

———. "Economic Anxieties Bring Debate on Immigration to a Boil." *Congressional Quarterly Weekly Report,* 16 March 1996: 701.

———. "House Judiciary Approves Sweeping Restrictions," *Congressional Quarterly Weekly Report,* 28 October 1995: 3305.

"Immigration Reform Dies at Session's End." *1984 Congressional Quarterly Almanac:* 232.

"Immigration Reform Measure Dies in House." *1982 Congressional Quarterly Almanac:* 407.

Ippolito, Dennis S., and Thomas G. Walker. *Political Parties, Interest Groups, and Public Policy: Group Influence in American Politics.* Englewood Cliffs, N.J.: Prentice Hall, 1980.

Kirk, Jim. "AFL-CIO Chief Backs Jobs Bill; Details Union Plans to Rainbow Coalition." *Chicago Sun-Times,* 2 March 1996: 28.

Kirk, Russell. *The Politics of Prudence.* Bryn Mawr, Pa.: Intercollegiate Studies Institute, 1993.

Kranish, Michael. "Clinton Policy Shift Followed Asian-American Fundraiser." *Boston Globe,* 15 January 1997: A1.

Lamm, Richard D., and Gary Imhoff. *The Immigration Time Bomb.* New York: Truman Talley Books, 1985.

Lazo, Robert. "Latinos and the AFL-CIO: The California Immigrant Workers Association as an Important New Development." Antoinette Sedillo Lopez, ed. *Latino Employment, Labor Organizations and Immigration.* New York: Garland Publishing, 1995.

Lee, Kenneth. "Hasta La Vista." *New Republic,* 27 October, 1997: 13–14.

———. "Let's Sell More U.S. Visas." *American Enterprise,* March/April 1997: 76.

LeMay, Michael C. *From Open Door to Dutch Door: An Analysis of U.S. Immigration Policy since 1820.* New York: Praeger, 1987.

———. "U.S. Immigration Policy and Politics." Michael C. LeMay, ed. *The Gatekeepers: Comparative Immigration Policy.* New York: Praeger, 1989.

Lindblom, Charles. *Politics and Markets: The World's Political-Economic Systems.* New York: Basic Books, 1977.

Lowi, Theodore J. *The End of Liberalism: The Second Republic of the United States.* 2d ed. New York: W. W. Norton & Company, 1979.

———. *The End of the Republican Era.* Norman: University of Oklahoma Press, 1995.

Lyons, Richard D. "Seldom Active Senate Unit Drew $2–Million in Decade." *New York Times,* 29 September 1975: 1.

Masci, David. "Panel OKs Restrictions on Legal Immigrants." *Congressional Quarterly Weekly Report,* 2 December 1995: 3656.

Mashberg, Tom. "Crossing the Boundaries—Politicians Haggle on the Future of Immigration." *Boston Herald,* 20 October 1996: 5.

McCloskey, Robert G., and Sanford Levinson. *The American Supreme Court* 2d ed. Chicago: The University of Chicago Press, 1994.

Miliband, Ralph. *The State in Capitalist Society.* New York: Basic Books, 1969.

Mills, C. Wright. *The Power Elite.* New York: Oxford University Press, 1959.

Morris, Milton D. *Immigration—The Beleaguered Bureaucracy.* Washington, D.C.: Urban Institute Press, 1985.

Ornstein, Norman, and Shirley Elder. *Interest Groups, Lobbying and Policymaking.* Washington, D.C.: Congressional Quarterly Press, 1978.

Page, Benjamin I., and Robert Y. Shapiro. "Effects of Public Opinion on Policy," *American Political Science Review* 22 (1983): 177.

Pear, Robert. "Congressional Inquiry Finds Aliens Getting Federal Subsidies for Rents." *New York Times,* 16 March 1981: A13.

Purdy, Matthew. "Unlikely Allies Battle Congress over Anti-Immigration Plans," *New York Times,* 11 October 1995: B1.

Reimers, David M. "Recent Immigration Policy: An Analysis." Barry R.
     Chiswick, ed. *The Gateway: U.S. Immigration Issues and Policies.*
     Washington, D.C.: American Enterprise Institute, 1982.
———. *Still the Golden Door: The Third World Comes to America.* New York:
     Columbia University Press, 1992.
Reinhold, Robert. "Flow of 3rd World Immigrants Alters Weave of U.S.
     Society." *New York Times,* 30 June 1986: A1.
Rivera-Batiz, Francisco L., Selig L. Sechzer, and Ira N. Gang. *U.S. Immigra-
     tion Policy Reform in the 1980s: A Preliminary Assessment.* New York:
     Praeger, 1991.
Roper Center at University of Connecticut Public Opinion Online.
Schmitt, Eric. "In Immigration Bill Debate, Divisions and Odd Alliances,"
     New York Times, 26 February 1996: A1.
Schuck, Peter H. "Overview: Domestic Implications of Immigration Policy."
     Yale Law & Policy Review 7 (1989): 1–19.
———. "The Politics of Rapid Legal Change: Immigration Policy in the
     1980s," pp. 47–87. Marc K. Landy and Martin A. Levin, eds. *The
     New Politics of Public Policy.* Baltimore: Johns Hopkins University
     Press, 1995.
Simcox, David E. *U.S. Immigration in the 1980s: Reappraisal and Reform.*
     Boulder. Colo.: Westview Press, 1988.
Simon, Julian. *The Economic Consequences of Immigration.* New York: B.
     Blackwell, 1989.
Simon, Rita J., and Susan H. Alexander. *The Ambivalent Welcome: Print
     Media, Public Opinion and Immigration.* New York: Praeger, 1993.
Skocpol, Theda. *Bringing the State Back.* Cambridge: Cambridge University
     Press, 1985.
Swartz, Rick. Private strategy memos and personal correspondence for the
     1990 and 1996 immigration bills. From the Office of Rick Swartz &
     Associates.
Tichenor, Daniel J. "The Politics of Immigration Reform in the United
     States, 1981–1990." *Polity* 26 (1994): 333–63.
Truman, David. *The Governmental Process.* New York: Knopf, 1951.
U.S. Commission on Immigration Reform. *Legal Immigration: Setting Pri-
     orities.* Washington, D.C.: U.S. Commission on Immigration Re-
     form, 1995.
———. *U.S. Immigration Policy: Restoring Credibility.* Washington, D.C.:
     U.S. Commission on Immigration Reform, 1994.
U.S. Congress. House Committee on Immigration and Naturalization. *Bio-
     logical Aspects of Immigration: Hearings,* 66th Congress, 2d Session,
     1921.
———. *Japanese Immigration: Hearings,* 66th Congress, 2d Session, 1921.

U.S. Congress. House Committee on the Judiciary. *Family Unity and Employment Opportunity Immigration Act of 1990*, 101st Congress, 2d Session, 1990, H. Rept. 101–723.

———. *Immigration Control and Legislation Amendments Act of 1986*, 99th Congress, 2d Session, 1986, H. Rept. 99–682.

———. *Immigration in the National Interest Act of 1995*, 104th Congress, 2d Session, 1995, H. Rept. 104–469.

———. *Immigration Reform and Control Act of 1982*, 97th Congress, 2d Session, 1982, H. Rept. 97–890.

———. *Immigration Reform and Control Act of 1983*, 98th Congress, 1st Session, 1983, H. Rept. 98–115.

U.S. Congress. House Subcommittee on Immigration and Claims of the Committee on the Judiciary. *Immigration in the National Interest Act of 1995: Hearings*, 104th Congress, 1st Session, 1995.

U.S. Congress. House Subcommittee on Immigration, Refugees and International Law of the Committee on the Judiciary. *Immigration Act of 1989 (Part 1): Hearings*, 101st Congress, 1st Session, 1989.

———. *Immigration Act of 1989 (Part 2): Hearings*, 101st Congress, 2d Session, 1989.

U.S. Congress. House Subcommittee on Immigration, Refugees and International Law of the Committee on Judiciary, and Immigration Task Force of the Committee on Education and Labor. *Immigration Act of 1989 (Part 3): Hearings*, 101st Congress, 2nd Session, 1989.

U.S. Congress. Senate Committee on the Judiciary. *Immigration Act of 1989*, 101st Congress, 1st Session, 1989, S. Rept. 101–55.

———. *Immigration Control and Financial Responsibility Act of 1996*, 104th Congress, 2d Session, 1996, S. Rept. 104–249.

———. *Immigration Reform and Control*, 97th Congress, 2d Session, 1982, S. Rept. 97–485.

———. *Legal Immigration Act of 1996*, 104th Congress, 2d Session, 1996, S. Rept. 104–250.

U.S. Immigration and Naturalization Service. *Statistical Yearbook of the Immigration and Naturalization Service, 1994*. Washington, D.C.: U.S. Government Printing Office, 1996.

U.S. Select Commission on Immigration and Refugee Policy (SCIRP). *U.S. Immigration Policy and the National Interest: The Final Report and Recommendations of the Select Commission on Immigration and Refugee Policy with Supplemental Views by Commissioners*. Washington, D.C.: U.S. Government Printing Office, 1981.

Wanta, Wayne, and Yu-Wei Hu. "Time-Lag Differences in the Agenda-Setting Process: An Examination of Five News Media." *International Journal of Public Opinion Research* 6 (1994): 225–240.

Wattenberg, Ben J. *The First Universal Nation: Leading Indicators and Ideas about the Surge of America in the 1990s.* New York: The Free Press, 1991.

Will, George. "Liberals, Racism and Asian-Americans." *St. Louis Post-Dispatch,* 18 April 1989: 3B.

Williamson, Chilton, Jr. *The Immigration Mystique: America's False Conscience.* New York: Basic Books, 1996.

SELECTED INTERVIEWS

Briggs, Vernon, Jr. (Labor economist, Cornell University), 3/31/97.

Brooks, Sylvia (President of Houston Urban League), 2/97.

Dyess, Kirby (Vice President of Human Resources, Intel Corporation), 8/96.

Eide, Peter (Chamber of Commerce lobbyist), 4/4/97.

Garling, Skip (Director of Research and Publications, Federation for American Immigration Reform), 4/11/97.

Kwok, Daphne (Organization of Chinese Americans), 4/2/97 and 4/4/97.

McAlpine, Robert (Washington Director of Public Policy, National Urban League), 2/97.

Pritchard, David (Director of Recruiting, Microsoft Corporation), 8/96.

Simpson, Alan (former Senator, R-Wyo.), 4/11/97.

Smith, Lamar (Congressman, R-Tex.), 3/31/97.

Swartz, Rick (Immigration lobbyist), 3/31/97 and 4/2/97.

Index

About the Author

KENNETH K. LEE, a free-lance writer, has written on immigration and other issues for various publications, including *The New Republic*, *The American Enterprise*, *Los Angeles Times*, *Orange County Register*, *Heterodoxy*, and *Liberty*.